THE TECHNIQUES of ASTRAL PROJECTION

by

Dr. Douglas Baker
B.A., M.R.C.S., L.R.C.P.

Drawings by
Pat Ludlow

First Published: 1969
This Edition (Revised & Updated): 1995

ISBN: 0 906006 89 9

Printed and Published in England by
**Baker Publications
Little Elephant
High Road
Essendon
Herts
AL9 6HR**

Copyright © 1995 D.M.Baker

*This book is gratefully dedicated
to
David & Laurel Zimmerman*

CONTENTS

Foreword 7

1 The Nature of Astral Projection 11
  Nomenclature 13
  The Silver Cord 20
  Historic Examples 23
  Materialisation 28
  Is There a Scientific Rationale? 29
  Clairvoyance and Projection 30
  Projection and Telepathy 32

2 Types and Stages of Astral Projection 35
  The First Stage of Astral Projection 37
  The Second Stage of Astral Projection 40
  A Strong Desire Factor in Projection 40
  The Third Stage of Astral Projection 42
  The Fourth Stage of Astral Projection 44
  The Fifth Stage of Astral Projection 52

3 The Techniques 57
  Technique For Projecting to Stage One 59
  Technique for Projecting to Stage Two 62
  Technique for Projecting to Stage Three 64
  Some Examples 70
  Technique for Projecting to Stage Four 71
  Technique for Projecting to Stage Five 80

4 The Astral World 83
  The Sexual Factor in Projection 96

Important Foreword to this Edition

The techniques outlined in this work have been evolved through personal experience and research over the past 40 years. As a qualified doctor of medicine I can vouch for their safety—they are based on a simple process of taking an ordinary capacity or power, latent or manifesting within us and expanding and amplifying it so that it can be a device for securing out-of-body experience.

At that time, 40 years ago, the subject was extremely clandestine. Few people knew what an out-of-body experience (OBE) really was. Today, the whole field of investigation into this subject has exploded. Several notable books have been written on the subject of OBE's and public awareness of the phenomena is widespread. The tremendous advances in clinical medicine, which have accompanied technological innovation, have contributed to the increased awareness of OBE's. People suffering a sudden stroke or heart attack, whether in the High Street or on the operating table, are more likely to be revived. This has caused the medical establishment to reassess the clinical definition of death. Paramedics are so efficient in resuscitating the victims of such medical emergencies that expanding numbers recover and bring back with them compelling accounts of experiences they had during the crucial minutes that the heart had stopped and they were, what until recently would have been considered, clinically dead. It is called the near death experience and is characterised by an accompanying transformative vision. The vision is something so powerful that it is indelibly stamped on their consciousness for the rest of their days and has a transformative effect on their attitude to death and in the way they subsequently live.

Near Death experiences are only one aspect of OBE's. Spontaneous projections either from the dream state in what has been erroneously called 'lucid dreaming', or as the result of a sudden shock are also being increasingly reported. A long-standing friend of mine recently had an OBE that is typical of this type:

> "I was walking along New Malden High Street on the way to a hairdressing appointment. I was late and in a hurry. As I drew near the hairdressers, situated on the opposite side of the road, I turned to cross the High Street. As I approached the far curb I noticed a disturbance behind me. I did not have the time to go back to see what had happened so continued. I went a little further when I heard a voice that said: *'No, you must go back'*. Suddenly I was aware of lying on the ground looking up at a ring of faces.
>
> I found out later that, as I started to cross the High Street, I had been hit by a cyclist who I had not seen coming, and knocked unconscious. *I had been the cause of the disturbance I had seen behind me!* I waited for an ambulance, was taken to the local casualty and treated for cuts and bruises."

These many factors have contributed to a focusing of attention not only onto the whole subject of out-of-body experience but also the more complicated matter of deliberately leaving the physical body at will and projecting it to different parts of the astral world. In the orient, Tibet for instance, the capacity to use astral projection effectively in the spiritual life was considered to be a very rare and powerful feature of spiritual growth usually possessed only by a Master of the Wisdom. It was called 'Tulku' and is referred to in the works of H.P. Blavatsky. The increasing numbers of people reporting OBE's, however, no matter what name may be given to it by the scientific establishment, indicates that this latent capacity is rapidly emerging in the consciousness of humanity. This is one of the many and diverse expressions of the coming in of the Age of Aquarius and constitutes the beginnings of the New Religions that have been promised in esoteric literature for that time. These New Religions will be based on personal and direct experiences of the presence of spiritual beings and working in harmony with the natural laws and powers of nature.

— Douglas Baker
Little Elephant,
July 1995.

1

THE NATURE OF ASTRAL PROJECTION
What Astral Projection Is and Is Not

THE NATURE OF ASTRAL PROJECTION

We live at a time when increasing numbers of people are having out-of-body experiences. Many of them are young. Most often they are teenagers. Some of their experiences result from the taking of psychedelic drugs. More often it is because they are psychic in some way. We overlook the fact that this is an Age in which the young people of today are far more spiritually developed than their parents. Such precocious spirituality is typical of any New Age.

This phenomenon will go on increasing as the Age of Aquarius blossoms. More especially has it been accelerated in the period of 1975 to 2000 for, in this twenty five years, as predicted, the mysteries are being restored and an effort by five great Masters of the Wisdom is in progress.

When such young people tell their psychiatrists of their out-of-body experiences, they get little understanding in return. They are told that their experiences are hallucinatory and should be ignored and even avoided. But to thousands of mankind, out-of-body experiences are not confused with dreams and hallucinations. There is a tremendous difference. Out-of-body means just that. The physical body was left behind in bed whilst the consciousness dwelt in some other vehicle of consciousness, usually a replica of the physical but far more ethereal or ephemeral. Such is the reality of the experience that no other possible interpretation for it can be given by the one experiencing it than that of astral projection, i.e. projection away from the physical body in an astral body.

Nomenclature

It is difficult to describe what happens in adequate language. The writer has had many thousands of astral projections and knows the procedures well enough, but, nevertheless, must often falter in his explanations for lack of suitable nomenclature.

He has had to resort sometimes herein to the use of words associated with Yoga and with Theosophy because no others exist in English. But these words are restricted to a minimum.

There is another group of people having out-of-body experiences which is worth mentioning. It is those rare individuals who suffer clinical death. During a heart attack or whilst undergoing surgery, someone occasionally 'dies'. By this, we mean that the heart stops and to all intents and purposes, the person is dead. If or when he is successfully resuscitated, he frequently reports an out-of-body experience which is astral projection pure and simple, whilst the physical body lies 'dead' on the operating table.

Leslie Sharpe, a Toronto businessman had just this experience. Late one spring afternoon in 1970, his heart stopped beating and for three minutes and eleven seconds, he was 'dead'. But he survived and recalled, in vivid detail, his sensations during clinical death. I quote now from the report by the Toronto Daily Star columnist Sidney Katz:

> "Upon recovering consciousness, the first thing he told the doctor at his bedside was: 'If I go out again, don't bring me back it's so beautiful out there . . .
>
> I saw myself leave my body, coming out through my head and shoulders. The body was somewhat transparent, although not exactly in vapour form. Watching, I thought, *So this is what happens when you die'.*
>
> The scene suddenly shifted and Sharpe now found himself sitting on a small object, tilted at a 45° angle, travelling through a blue-grey sky at a great speed.
>
> The next sensation was of a *delightful floating* in a bright yellow light. Sharpe recalled: 'I have a scar on my right leg, the result of an old injury. Although, at the time, I was

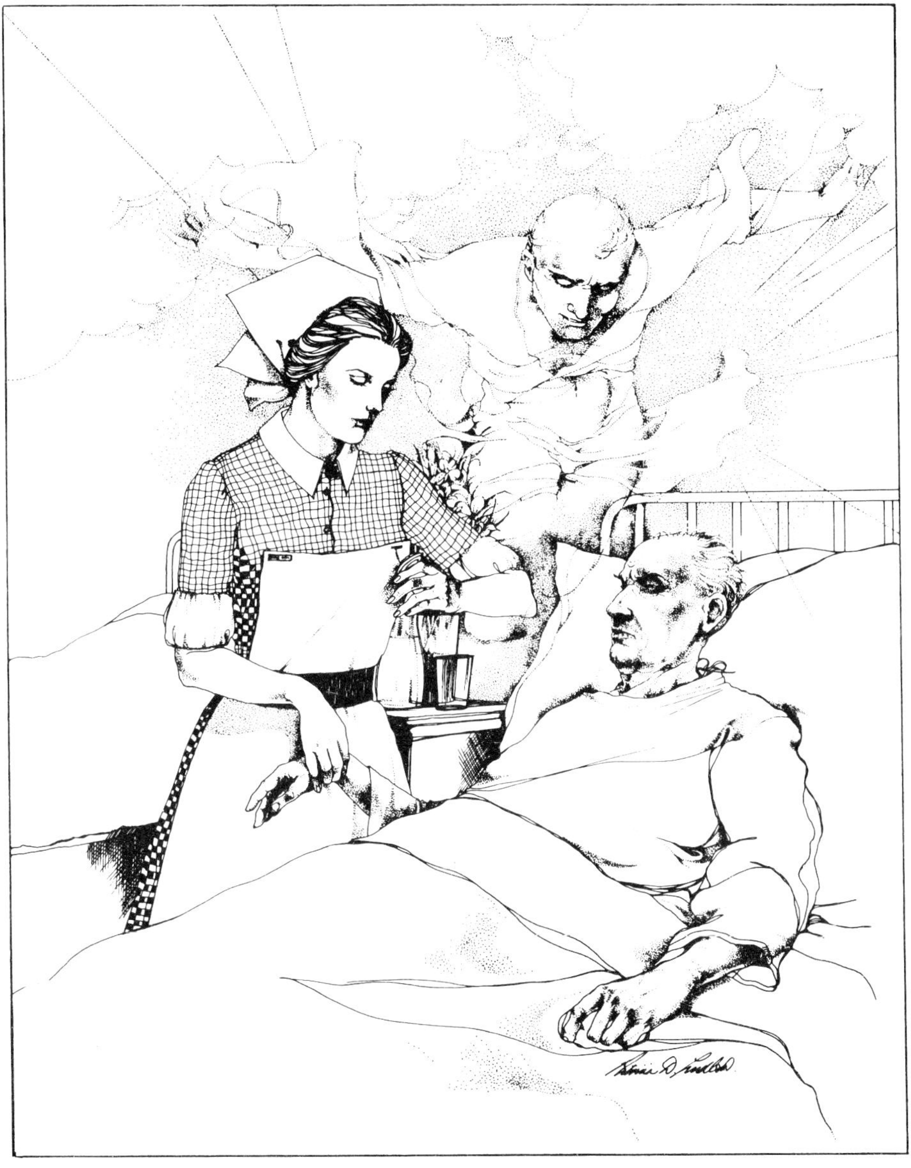

not conscious of having any lower limbs, I felt the scar being torn away and I thought *They have always said that your body is made whole out here. I wonder if my scars are gone?*

I tried unsuccessfully to locate my legs. In the meantime, I continued to float, enjoying the most beautiful, tranquil sensation. I have never experienced such a delightful sensation and have no words to describe it.'

Then a series of hard blows to his left side brought him back to consciousness. (His heart had been restarted by means of shocks from an electric paddle.) Looking up, he could recognise the doctors and nurses. They explained that he had taken a bad turn."

Leslie Sharpe's experience contains many elements of astral projection which provide important keys to the understanding of the phenomenon. Firstly, he insists that he was in another body. He also describes how that body had a sensory equipment of its own which did not detract from his having sensations in his more solid body lying, as it was, in bed. He had dual sensory equipment. His physical body possessed sensation and his astral body also had sensory equipment. For the student of astral projection, this is most important to understand. He must be prepared for this duality of sensation experienced in two different vehicles of consciousness. *The astral double possesses its own organs of sensation.* The great New York medium and clairvoyant Eileen Garrett often stressed this in connection with her astral projections:

"While I am in a state of projection, the double is apparently able to use the normal activity of all five senses which work in my physical body. For example, I may be sitting in the drawing room on a snowy day and yet be able in projection to reach a place where summer is at the moment full-blown. In that instant, I can register with all my five physical senses the sight of the flowers and the sea; I can smell the scent of the blossoms and the tang of the ocean spray, and hear the birds sing and the waves beat against the shore. Strange to say, I never forget the smallest detail of any such experience which has come to me through conscious projection, though in ordinary daily living I can be quite forgetful, and memories of places and things may grow dim."

The mechanism whereby one gains impressions of the inner worlds and of physical places a great distance away, is through the etheric centres or chakras. These are shown allied to their respective senses and psychic powers in the diagram from *The Etheric Double* by Major A.E. Powell. (See illustration over).

One is not likely to confuse the two bodies so far described. The physical body is interpenetrated and surrounded by a force-field most generally called The Etheric Body or double. This is a vehicle of subtle matter made of a material that interpenetrates any gas, liquid or solid just as easily as water interpenetrates sand. The etheric body has its own organs which are adequately described in any textbook of Theosophy. It energises the physical tissues and therefore, cannot be separated from the physical body for long. Dislodgement of the etheric matrix soon brings death to the overlying physical body. It cannot be projected.

On the other hand, the astral body is projected almost every time we go to sleep. When we enter the sleep state, we are usually still very active emotionally or astrally. We possess, as part of our normal equipment both an emotional body which is termed the astral in esoteric parlance and we also have a mental body.

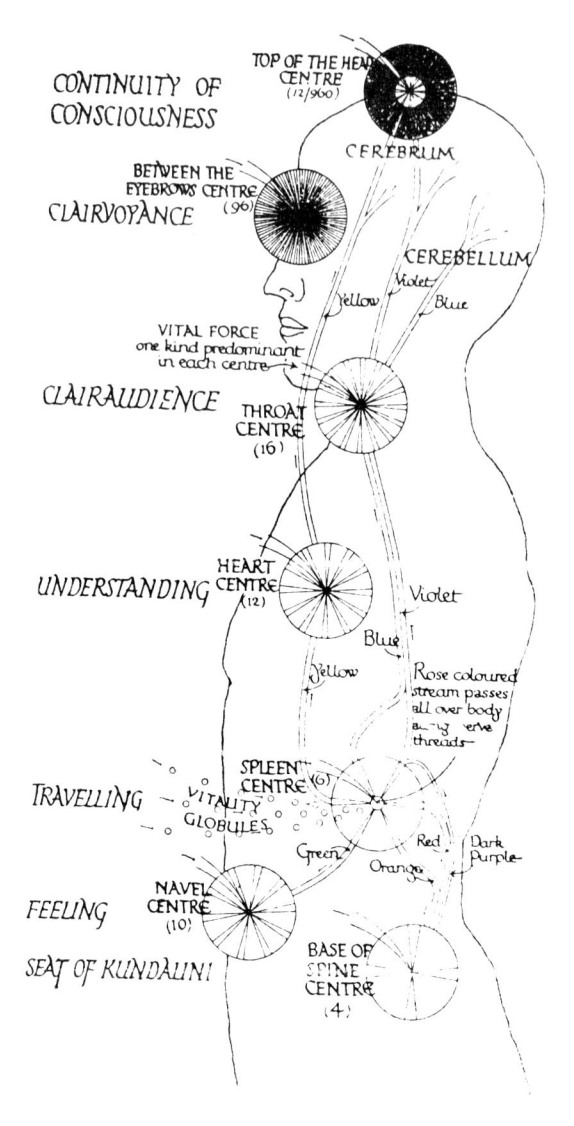

The diagram is of special interest here because it shows the pathways of vitality energising the centres with the energy of prana derived mainly from breath. (In the section on Techniques, we shall be referring to the importance of breathing in relation to astral activity.)

Higher Mental and Spiritual Bodies

Astral Body (Emotional)

Physical Body

Etheric Body (Surround)

These are both made up of matter even subtler than the etheric already described. When we think we act mentally in our mental bodies. The astral body is made up of finer substance than the etheric body but not as fine a material as that of the mental body.

In sleep, we slip out of the etherico-physical body and dwell in our astral and mental bodies. In these, especially the astral body, we tend to move about in the astral world which is almost an exact replica of those places we visit in waking consciousness but with reservations to this description which the writer describes at the end of this work.

When we awaken, the astral and mental bodies slip back into their usual position in close alignment with the physical and etheric bodies.

The Silver Cord

Sooner or later, one hears about a so-called silver cord that connects the astral double to its physico-etheric body. I mention the phenomenon here because many people aspiring to astral projection worry about this cord. It is said that the cord is made of a silver like material and so long as it is patent, the astral body will always return to its physical counterpart when we are awakened or return to our physical habitat.

There is also the suggestion that if the cord were to snap, return would not be possible. This becomes a real fear to many. In my own instance, many years back, I used to lock my bedroom door before any sort of esoteric endeavour like meditation or astral projection because of this fear.

It was widely believed that any sort of interruption whilst out of the body could bring about rupture of the silver cord.

Does it exist? Is there any danger linked to its breakage?

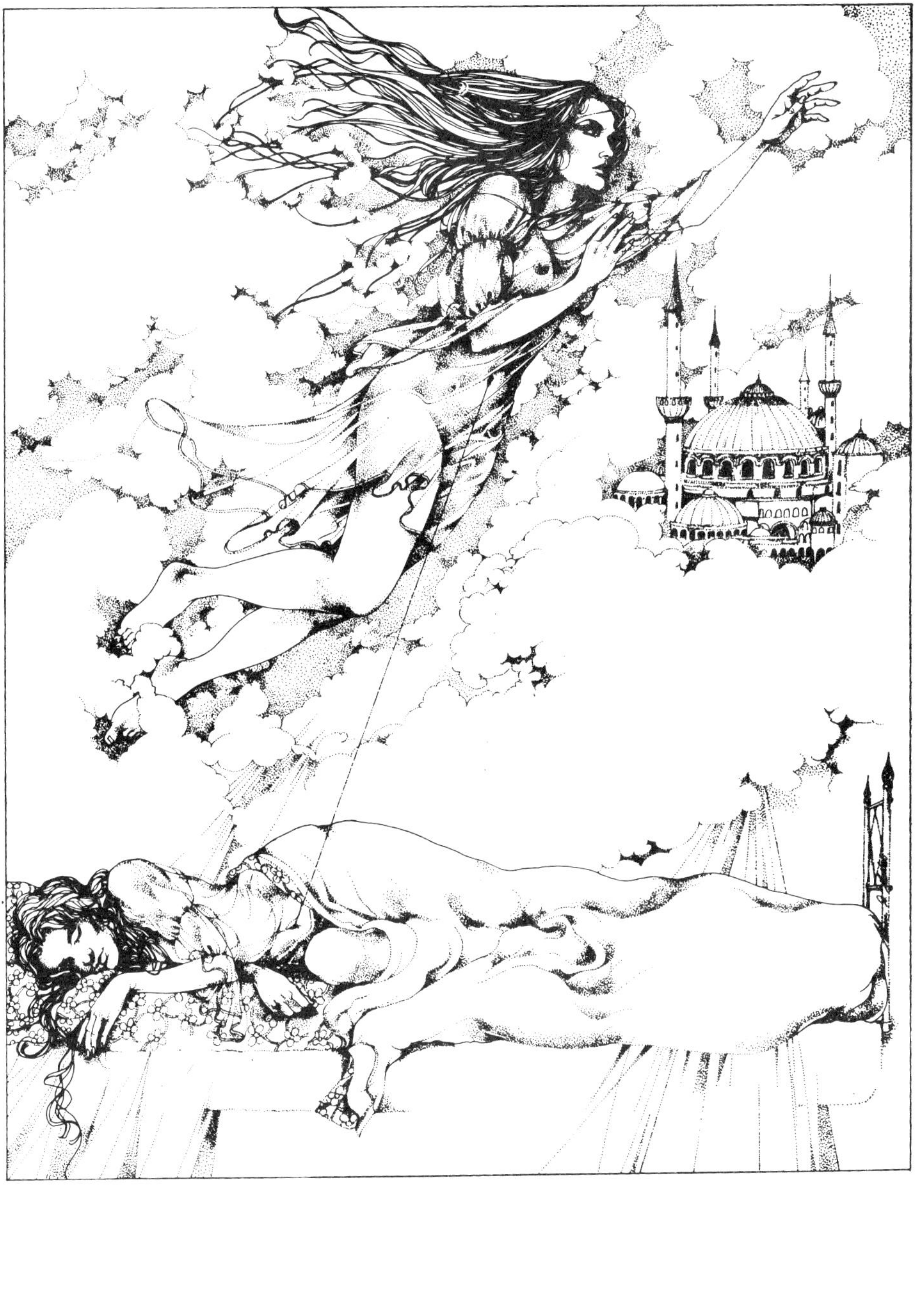

I can only speak from experience. In all my many projections, I have never seen a cord, either linked to me or to another person. This does not mean that the cord does not exist. It may be that with my nasty scientific mind, I don't or won't accept that a piece of material like the so-called astral cord can be extended indefinitely, perhaps as much as two hundred thousand miles, say, to the Moon. That there is a tug back towards the physical body, I admit. That there is a feeling of linkage near the umbilicus or, in women, as Eileen Garrett describes it, just above the breasts, I will also admit, but that it is a cord, I will not accept. I always say:

"If you see a cord, take a pair of scissors and cut it!"

The great mystics and mediums who have all practised projection of some sort do not seem to have left behind them descriptions of physical responses to astral projection even though some of them were medically trained.

My own experiences confirm what little information we have gleaned from various records.

Swedenborg was also in his earlier days a profound student of anatomy and physiology and he frequently gave valuable information about his own clinical condition during periods of mystical insight. But there is practically nothing in his work describing his symptoms during astral travel. On the other hand, Eileen Garrett clearly describes the mechanism of astral projection she used and the accompanying physical sensations and symptoms, which to me, also one who has consciously projected my consciousness to distances in my astral vehicle, are almost identical:

"What is generally accepted by science," she says, "but which I, nevertheless, know to be true, is that everyone has a double of finer substances than the physical body; it is referred to either as the astral or as the etheric body by some scientists. This is not to be confused with the surround which remains in position enveloping the human body, while the double can be projected. It is by means of this double that either accidental or conscious projection is accomplished. Now in these experiments, I was doing conscious projection, and I know from my own experience that when I project this double, I do so from the centre of my chest above the breasts. From the moment I begin to project, I am aware at this point of a pull, accompanied by a fluttering, which causes the heart to palpitate, and the breathing to speed up, accompanied also, if the projection is a long one, by a slight choking in the larynx and a heady sensation. As long as the projection continues, I remain aware of these sensations taking place in my physical body."

But before we consider variations to astral projection and what astral projection is not, let us look at some interesting historical examples of the phenomenon.

Historic Examples

Anyone acquainted with Jewish history will recall an occasion when the council chamber of Ben-hadad, King of Syria, was invaded by the spirit, or subconscious of a Jewish prophet. Every time the king had attempted a raid on Israel, he found that his plans had been betrayed to his intended victim, and in despair, he cried, "Will ye not show me which of us is for the King of Israel?" "None, my Lord, O King," was the reply, "but Elisha, the prophet that is in Israel, telleth the King of Israel the words that thou speakest in thy bedchamber." The prophet's astral body had journeyed to Damascus with the physical still in Israel.

◆

Probably many of the siddhis of the saints concerned with the phenomenon of levitation which was almost commonplace in medieval times, were really manifestations of an astral body arriving or leaving, miles away from its physical counterpart.

◆

It is related that St. Anthony of Padua, when preaching in the Church of St. Pierre de Quayroix at Limoges on Holy Thursday in 1226, suddenly remembered that he was due at that hour for a service in a monastery at the other end of town.

Drawing his hood over his head, he knelt down for some minutes while the congregation reverently waited. At that moment, the saint was seen by the assembled monks to step forth from his stall in the monastery chapel, read the appointed passage in the Office, and immediately disappear.

◆

A similar experience is recorded of St. Severus of Ravenna, St. Ambrose and St. Clement of Rome.

◆

At a later date, September 17th, 1174, Alphonse de Lignori, when imprisoned in Arezzo, remained for five days in his cell without taking nourishment. Awakening one morning at the end of his fast, he declared that he had been present at the deathbed of Pope Clement XIV. His statement was subsequently confirmed, for he had been seen in attendance at the bedside of the dying pope.

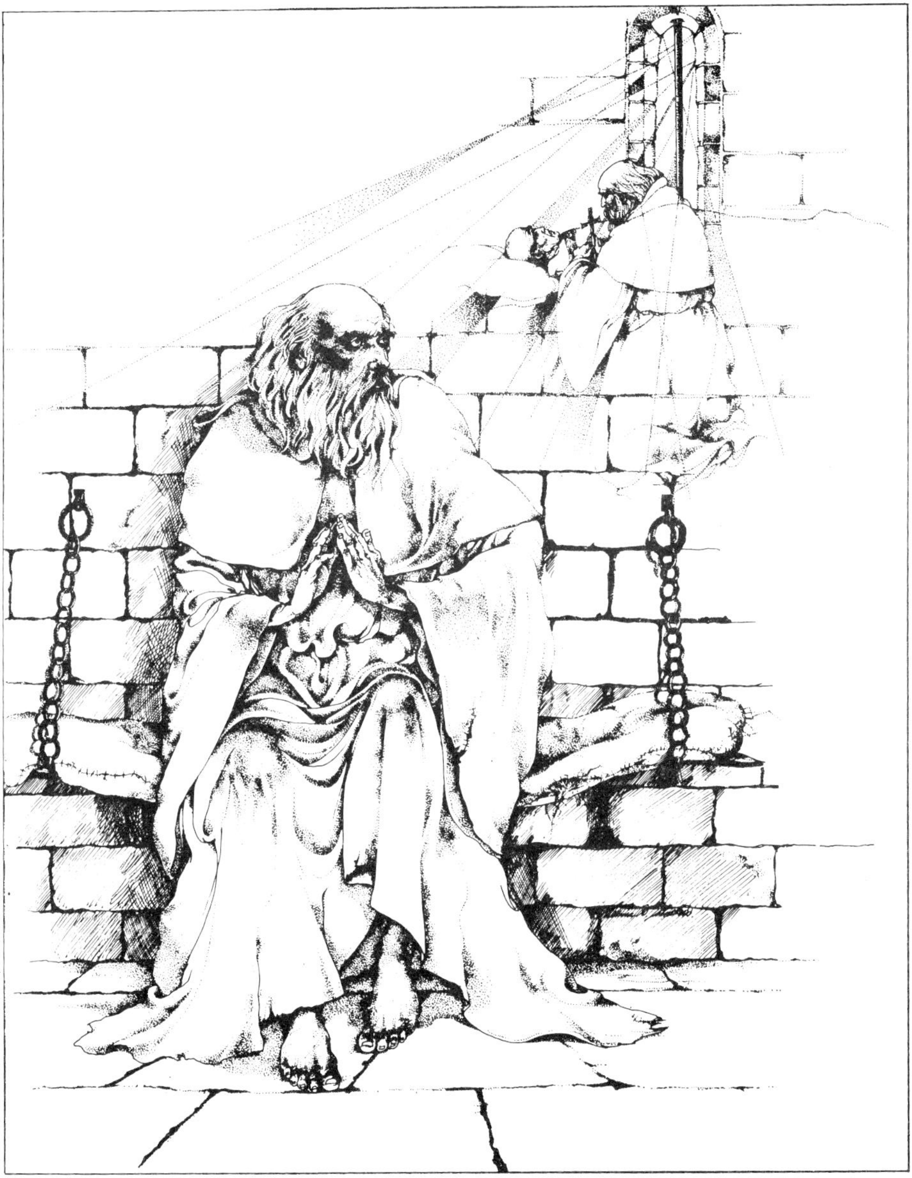

What more respectable examples could we take than those astral projections which were made into the British House of Commons and witnessed by eminent members there? There are numerous historic examples.

◆

Sir Carne Rasch, when ill in bed, was seen in the House of Commons by Sir Gilbert Parker and also by Sir Arthur Hayter. Describing the incident, Sir Gilbert said, "When Rasch accepted my nod with what looked very much like a glare, and met my kindly enquiry with silence, I was a little surprised". He went on to explain that, when his friend's figure suddenly and silently vanished, he felt convinced that what he had seen was a ghost, and that Rasch must have succumbed to his illness. Sir Arthur Hayter, who also greeted the figure, was just as positively persuaded that he had seen Sir Carne, was struck by his extreme pallor, and noticed that he occupied a seat remote from his accustomed place.

◆

Dr. Mark Macdonnell was another who, while ill in bed, appeared in the House, was seen by fellow Members on two consecutive days and actually entered the Division lobby and recorded his vote.

◆

J.G. Swift McNeill, M.P., recounted how, in 1897, the double of T.P. O'Connor was seen in the House of Commons in his wonted place while he was on his way to Ireland to take a last farewell of a dying parent.

◆

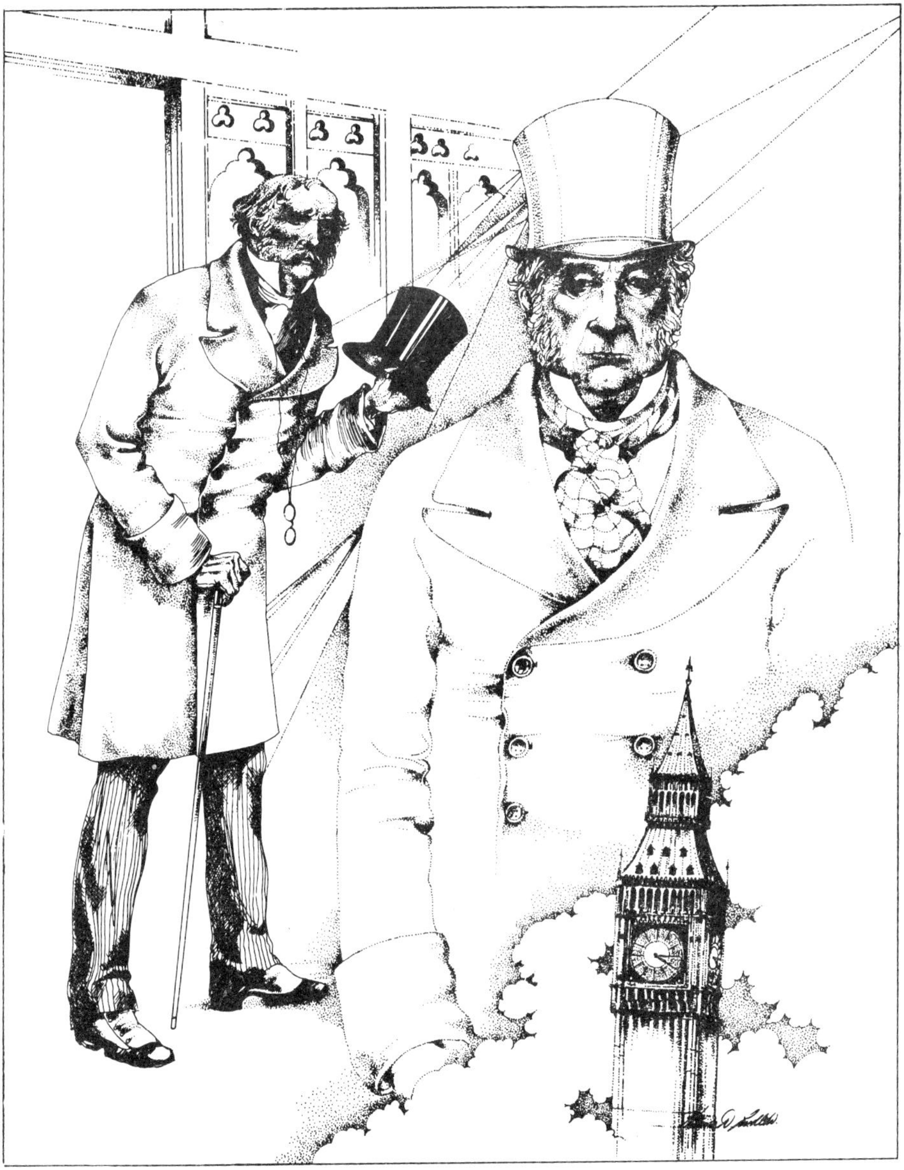

The case of Dr. Macdonnell did, indeed, come in for a certain amount of comment in the Press, but seems not even to have been a nine day's wonder.

Materialisation

In all these latter examples of astral projection, there has been a complicating factor which introduces the subject of materialisation. The examples are given to emphasise that there is reality about projection. But this was because the projection ended in materialisation of the individual. He was seen because his astral body had materialised, if only for a short time.

This is not the place to go into the whole subject of materialisation. Suffice is it to say that the human body gives off, in very small quantities, an ephemeral substance called ectoplasm. This is mainly albumin and some amino acids. It is secreted from the orifices of the body. One rare individual in about 50 million has the capacity to produce it in vast quantities especially during the trance state. This person would be known as a materialisation medium. Strong white light is antagonistic to the material which is best seen and gathered in conditions where red light is used. In a materialisation seance, huge amounts may be produced by the entranced medium and then it can act as a reservoir from which astral entities can draw upon it. They will then be able to materialise for all to see and will remain so until the ectoplasm supplies peter out. The writer has had much experience in investigating this phenomenon and would refer you to his work on the subject. Its relevance here is to astral projection.

Occasionally, when there is a supply of ectoplasm available, an astral body of someone in projection will materialise. This occurred, for example, in the episodes witnessed in the House of Commons.

Members there had, no doubt, 'donated' ectoplasm, willy nilly, to the astral body of their colleague, Sir Carne Rasch, when he projected into their midst. Old houses are saturated with ectoplasmic material and this provides the source of ghosts and wraiths seen in such places where astral forms, often earthbound by some tragic circumstances, draw on the environment for the means to materialise.

In situations which are relevant to our subject here, it would mean that when one projects to a place or a person where ectoplasm is available, materialisation of the astral form or just part of it, say a face or hand, would be possible. Sometimes, the one to whom the projection is made, may provide the ectoplasm, especially, it is said and with some truth, in the case of plump matrons!

Is There a Scientific Rationale?

Not until science is prepared to admit the existence of mental and emotional Matter will it be possible to prove the existence of an astral body and the capacity to direct it purposefully about some task. Everywhere, people are beginning to photograph thought and feeling.

The recent detection of *dark matter* by instruments in satellites orbiting the Earth suggests the re-discovery of what the 'Wisdom of the Ages' has proclaimed for many, many centuries – that there are subtle planes of material interpenetrating the solar system and its planets in which we all manifest elements of our consciousness in what we still call *bodies* and *vehicles*. Thus, the mental body gives us access to the mental planet interpenetrating the Earth and the astral body access to the astral world in OBE's, etc, etc.

Probably, however, the greatest 'breakthrough' will occur in the increasing ability of science to detect force-fields and radiations about living things, leading ultimately to an analysis of the fields into different types . . . ultimately into etheric, astral and mental, and (hopefully) spiritual.

I think that the comment by H.F. Prevost Battersby in his book, *Man Outside Himself*, is very relevant here:

> "Where the mystery of man's nature is concerned, we seem to be scientifically shy of expressing an opinion, and still more curiously averse from any effort to discover truth.
>
> We have no theories to account for such happenings, and we are apprehensive that discovery might imperil conclusions which have been worked into the fabric of our scientific faith. So we talk airily of thought-forms or hallucinations, and are content to leave it at that."

Clairvoyance and Projection

There is some confusion about clairvoyance and what is seen in astral projection. Clairvoyance may occur in astral projection when the projector reaches a 'target' which has a physical nature. Most targets do not. If one projects to the Taj Mahal, it would be possible to see what is occurring there. This would be clairvoyance with astral projection, but the energy expenditure in maintaining the projection would be prohibitive to do this very often. Clairvoyance without astral projection involves a different psychic capacity.

The great clairvoyance of Emanuel Swedenborg is often quoted as an example of astral projection but it was not astral projection. Swedenborg was in contact with an adept and any perusal of his spiritual diaries would confirm this. He was able to project but it should not be assumed that all clairvoyance implies that the consciousness is projected to the object of interest. This would negate the factor of astral light in which lie the akashic records, made use of so profusely by Madame Blavatsky and others.

The following account of a clairvoyant observation by Swedenborg is typical of the great Swedish mystic, a previous life of Eliphas Levi and a subsequent life of Paracelsus:

> Towards the end of September, 1756, Swedenborg had just landed at Gothenburg, where he had been invited to stay at the house of a friend, named Castel, along with a number of other guests.
>
> About six o'clock of the evening, he went out of the house returning somewhat later looking pale and much upset. Asked what troubled him, he explained that he had become conscious of a terrible fire that was raging in Stockholm three hundred miles away, which was increasing in violence at the very moment, and was causing him the greatest anxiety, as the house of one of his friends had already been destroyed and his own house was in danger.
>
> He thereupon went out again, and returning at eight o'clock exclaimed, "God be praised, the fire has been extinguished at the third house from my own!"

This statement, which caused an immense sensation, reached the Governor's ears the same evening, and the next day, Sunday, he sent for Swedenborg, who described for him the exact nature and extent of the conflagration, how it had begun and the time during which it had continued.

As the story spread, many of the citizens of Gothenburg were greatly concerned, having friends and property in Stockholm.

On Monday evening, official news was brought by a courier, who had been sent by the merchants of Stockholm during the fire.

The account he brought confirmed Swedenborg's statement in every particular, and a further courier, despatched by the King, arrived at the Governor's house on Tuesday morning, giving fuller details of the ravages of the conflagration, and further stating that it had been got under control at 8 p.m., the very hour which Swedenborg had reported.

In an age in which many religions are created and preached abroad, I wonder how many originators of them could claim the inner perception of Swedenborg and his knowledge of the higher worlds. Yet, Swedenborg's own new religion, incorporating the Church of the New Jerusalem, has been practically ignored by the world. Swedenborg was a true prophet, amongst an abundance of false ones.

Projection and Telepathy

There is one further point. The world has come to accept telepathy. Many universities have done extensive research work into this phenomenon and have shown that it is not an illusion. Thus, we accept that something can be transferred from one mind to another. What it is we don't know . . . a wavelength, a quantum of energy, or merely rapport. We accept this transfer. Is it then so difficult to accept that perhaps *something more* is also transferred . . . an agglomeration of particles of subtle matter which we call the astral body?

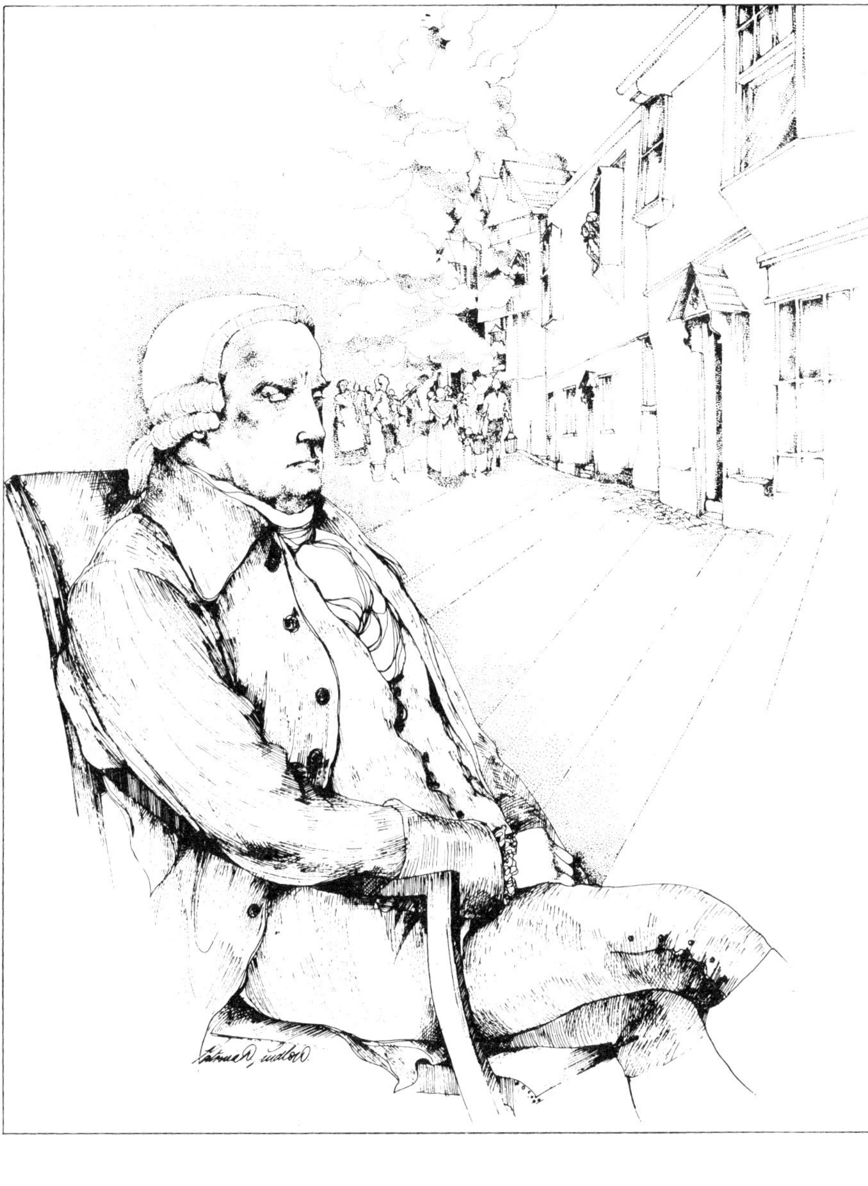

2

TYPES AND STAGES OF ASTRAL PROJECTION

TYPES AND STAGES OF ASTRAL PROJECTION

There are basically two types of astral projection. There is the projection which occurs whilst the subject is fully conscious and alert in his waking consciousness and there are projections which happen whilst the physical body is asleep or unconscious. The types dealt with in this work fall into the second category.

It is recommended that the techniques for developing projection from the waking state be left until sufficient expertise has been gained from projections had whilst the physical body is in repose or unconscious. The latter techniques are far safer and, in the opinion of the author, more likely to lead to fruitful results than the former. They are also highly related to spiritual development.

There are five stages described here. In the section that follows, we shall consider a technique for procuring each stage of projection. After each stage, now described, an example is given, either from the experience of the author or from famous occultists.

The First Stage of Astral Projection

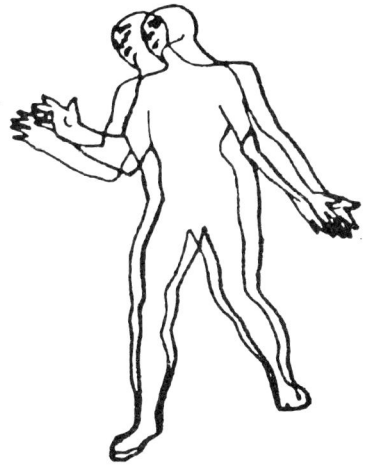

The astral body is put just out of alignment with the physical. This is the normal state of being for average man when he goes to sleep. In the sleep state, the astral body goes out of alignment with its physical counterpart. It is not possible to produce, by means of any drug or other device, the refreshing reward of a good night's sleep. In sleep, when the astral body slips out of close alignment with the physical body, all the inner vehicles become, as it were, *en rapport*. They quickly recharge themselves with the glorious energies which flow from the worlds within and when we awaken, we have not only the rewards which result from the resting of the metabolism of the physical body but emotional and mental vigour stemming from energies gained by our astral and mental bodies whilst they were, in sleep, out of alignment with the physical body.

In sleep, we all experience astral projection! Only some of us are aware of being out of our bodies in what we call vivid dreams. A very few of us are fully conscious, at times, whilst the physical is asleep. It is then that we are able to project.

In the section on techniques, we shall describe *how to project the astral body out of alignment in full consciousness and why this is recommendable,* the physical body being, of course, in deep repose at the time.

All of us have had experiences at some time or the other of being out of the physical body during sleep in *full consciousness.* Let me give an example of what more than sixty per cent of all audiences I have lectured to on this subject, have verified.

At some time or the other in your life, you must have performed some repetitive action involving intense and sustained physical action. Perhaps you have driven sixteen hours non-stop down winding country roads, negotiating bend after bend. Eventually worn-out, you reach your home. You drag yourself to your bedroom and, too tired to even change, you fling yourself down wearily on to your bed. But you find you cannot sleep. Your mind is still alert. You are back on that road negotiating the bends, speeding and braking. Your physical body is relaxed and virtually asleep! Suddenly, in your alert mind you steer too near the edge of the road. This traumatic inner experience shocks you and you suddenly jolt back into consciousness. *You have had a projection out of your exhausted physical body whilst your mind was awake! You have had a stage one astral projection in full consciousness.*

The violent jolt was said by Eileen Garrett to be the result of meeting with some obstruction in the astral world that forces us, traumatically back into alignment with the physical body. This may well be so.

It is important here to remember the state of the physical body which is usually exhausted or very negative at the time of the out-of-body experience. Later we shall see why.

I remember having such an experience as a boy after a long day pitching and tossing on board a yacht at sea. That evening, when trying to rest, I was again on the yacht and I was ducking to miss a swinging boom (without much success, I must say) that brought me jolting back into my physical body.

The use of anaesthetics pushes the astral body out of alignment. This may be a local phenomenon or the total body may be affected. Trilene gas, used in labour of childbirth, gives partial anaesthesia leaving the pregnant woman still conscious in what must be, technically speaking, partial stage one projection. But here, the focus on events in the room is so demanding that the phenomenon is overlooked.

In *sitting for development*, the same phenomenon occurs. In this situation, the subject has made himself very negative. He is receptive to any flow of energy or influence. The astral body is pulled towards more positive areas and leaves the physical body to become a vehicle for any other consciousnesses that would like to occupy it. This is called *sitting for development* and where the sitter is not under the care of a guru or a medium of many years experience, the practice may get out of hand so that slipping out of the body may become uncontrolled. This can lead to some forms of schizophrenia wherein possession by astral entities of a low order may result.

Air travel can force the inner vehicles out of alignment without bringing the refreshing rewards of the benefit of true sleep, but instead, only nervous and physical exhaustion.

I would issue a warning here to all those who sunbathe. It is extremely dangerous to sleep in the hot midday sun. In this state, the astral body is out of alignment and the physical body becomes the defenceless prey of the strong inflow of cosmic rays, without the buffering action of its inner vehicles to support the helpless physical tissues. This can lead to heatstroke and excessive sunburning.

The Second Stage of Astral Projection

The astral body is projected to a distance of some feet from its physical sheath. This phenomenon is frequently reported when questionnaires on psychic matters are sent out to the public. This stage of projection may occur through some trauma or accident. The person is struck by an automobile or slips down a mountainside. He finds himself outside his body. Sometimes he sees below him his physical body being tended to by nurses and doctors.

Under the heading of **Techniques**, we shall be considering how to project to this distance from the physical body in full waking consciousness but again with the physical body in repose.

In all the remaining stages of astral projection, the factor of desire now enters prominently and it would be advisable to go into the subject somewhat before proceeding further.

A Strong Desire Factor in Projection

Projection being basically astral or emotional in nature, requires a strong *desire factor* to be present. For most Westerners, the consciousness is oriented towards the Solar Plexus Chakram and the astral plane, most of us still being Atlantean in outlook. The power of strong desire to achieve its target both in the physical and astral world may be illustrated by an old tale that comes from somewhere in the near East. About the fifteenth century A.D., there grew into power a group of men who used political assassination as its method of replacing the existing order with its own henchmen. The leader had long plotted the downfall of one of the last potentates, a Caliph of a powerful city near the Persian Border. On every occasion, the best laid plans of assassination had failed to destroy the Caliph. Then one of the band hit upon a ruthless and diabolical plan to succeed where others had failed. A young and fiery soldier was enticed by the band to a tavern and was made very drunk. He was knocked over the head and carried off, unconscious, to their mountain hideout, a glorious castle, of white marble set high up in a gorge. In the palace gardens, the young soldier was revived and given every luxury. It soon became clear to him that he was in paradise and he thanked heaven for the tavern brawl that had deprived him of life and sent him to paradise. The strutting peacocks, the beauty of the women attendants and the servility of the proud men of the palace to his every whim settled him in for a thousand years in paradise.

But suddenly he was confronted by a sad story. He was told that a mistake had been made. He should never have died; paradise was not to be his yet. No amount of appeals could shake the resolution of those who conveyed the dismal tidings. He must go back and live out his miserable existence, unless . . . unless, they said, he would perform an act that would earn him death and paradise. What was the act? He must go to a nearby land where there lived a Caliph who had eluded the band's assassins. There he could murder the Caliph in exchange for a return to paradise.

The young man readily agreed, and having drunk a strong potion handed him by a fair maiden, he awoke once more in the tavern and found that he had been provided with a horse and arms. Despite the most appalling setbacks, injuries at the hands of the Caliph's guards, torture and even castration, he eventually succeeded.

There are two important points to be derived from this fable. Firstly, it illustrates that when desire is strong enough, it can overcome all obstacles and desire is the essence of the initial stages of astral projection. Secondly, it shows how a glimpse of a paradise or *a new world* can affect the outlook of anyone, and in the heights of astral projection, one can experience paradises that make the young man's castle in the clouds as nothing compared to them! Once they are visited, the desire to be back within them makes later astral projections easier.

The Third Stage of Astral Projection

The astral body is projected some distance, a few hundred feet or perhaps some miles, but always within familiar places. Now the element of desire enters. There is desire to be with some loved person or at some loved place, perhaps within the home or garden or nearby village. If the desire is strong enough, it may lead on to projection towards the object of the desire, or, what we may now refer to as the target. Under the occult law of *Energy Follows Thought*, the energy body which we call the astral, is strongly drawn towards the target or that which is desired or strongly thought about.

There is desire to be *with the target*, a loved one or a loved place and desire can be immensely powerful as we have already seen.

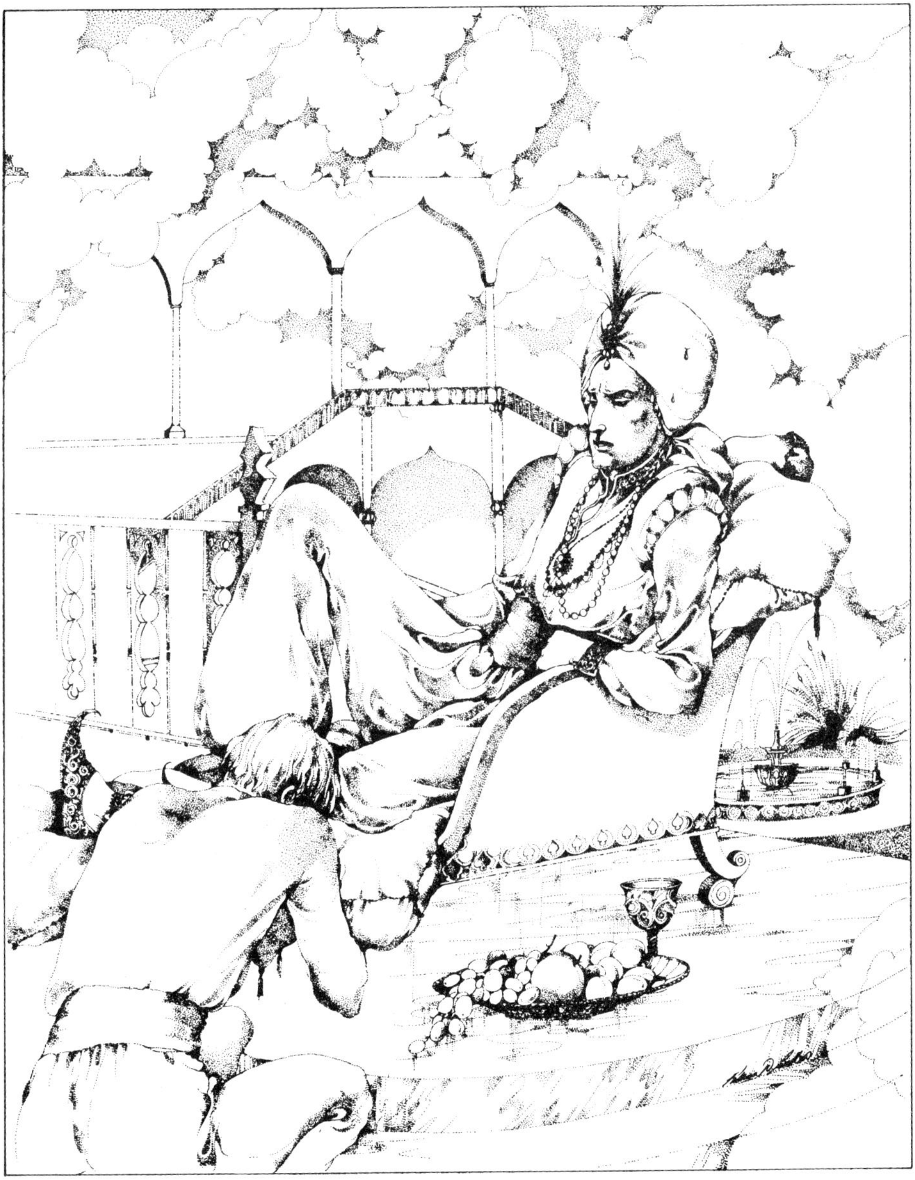

The example I quote for this stage of astral projection is from my own life. When I was at medical school as a student, I was once asked to lecture in a nearby city but this necessitated my having to stay overnight. I was perplexed because, though this was an engagement of long standing, a problem had meanwhile presented itself. My pet dog, a bitch Rhodesian Ridgeback had fallen pregnant. She was about to whelp and I did not want to leave her on her own. Fortunately, I was able to get a fellow-student to look after her. Accordingly, I bedded her down comfortably in my garage and went to my lecture. But I was still much concerned and that night, some miles away, I thought of her as I retired. I pictured her on her bed of straw and wondered whether she needed me. I must have fallen asleep for the next thing I knew, I was in my garage at home and there she was, lying quietly on her straw. I called to her and she came bounding towards me. I could see her physical body lying where she had left it and I noted that she had not yet whelped. I had projected to someone I loved. My desire to be with her had drawn me, that is, my desire body to her in a stage three type projection.

The Fourth Stage of Astral Projection

The astral body is projected to targets far distant. In this stage, the desire factor is present and strong but is overshadowed by the will. A powerful will is required to project the astral form over great distances. In the same way that etheric matter adheres and surrounds astral matter for projections of short distance, astral matter surrounds mental substance being projected. The distance to which the projection could be made would depend on the 'Ring-Pass-Not' of the projector. This in turn would depend on the degree of his spiritual development or the strength of his will. Those who are initiates of the Third Degree are lim-

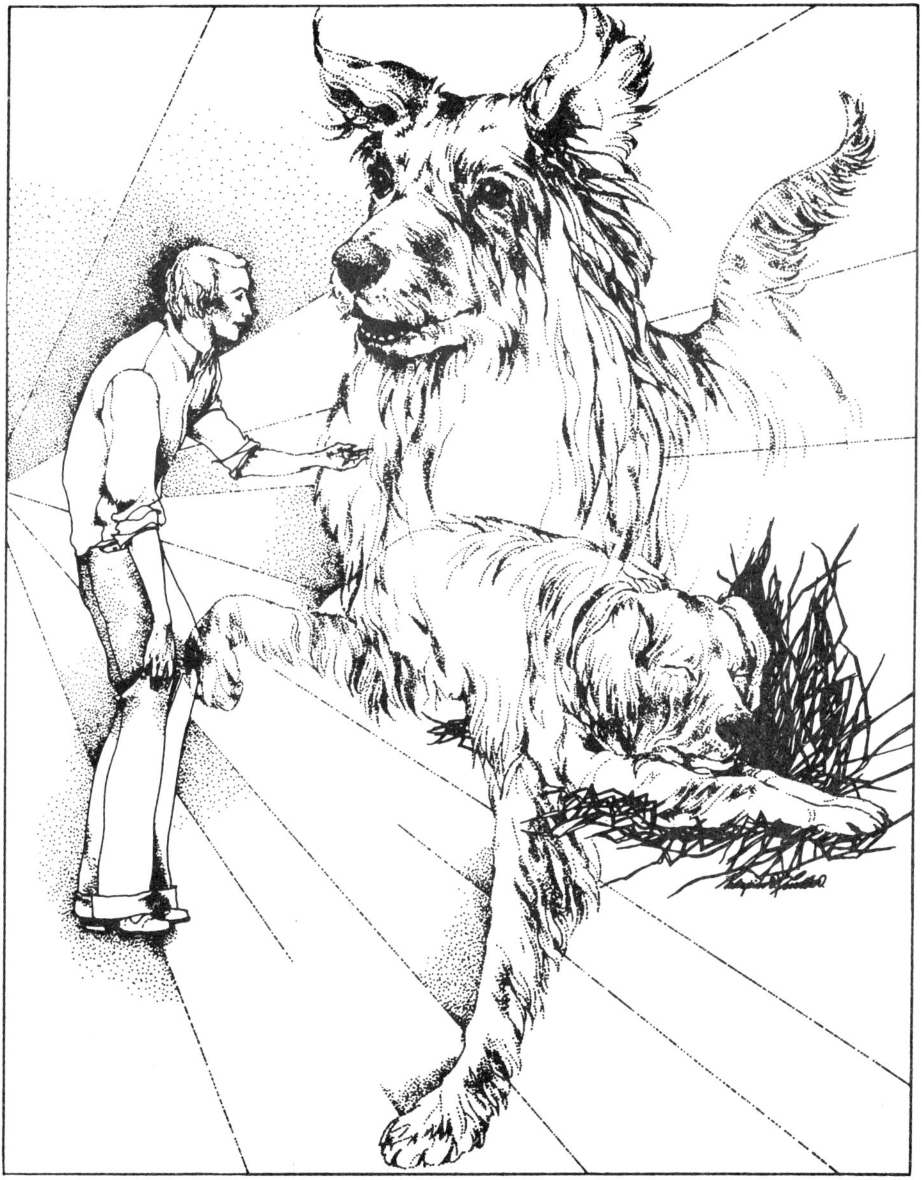

ited in their projections to a Ring-Pass-Not that extends a little way beyond the moon. Fourth degree initiates can reach the Sun. Fifth degree initiates (adepts and Masters) can reach to any part of the solar system and even as far as the great star Sirius.

In these projections which may be over immense distances, the astral body is supported by its mental counterpart and its impelling will. The physical body requires special treatment both to sustain it during the effort of mental extrusion and to maintain the projected astral body on target throughout the projections.

The projected bodies move fast. Some thousands of miles may be traversed in a matter of two or three seconds and the projector arrives at the target with such speed that sometimes he may, in the early stages of his training, experience a rebound phenomenon as he centres his astral body on target.

Mrs. Garrett's achievements in astral projection show to what heights this occult process may be brought in service work for the benefit of mankind. The following example illustrates just this and her capacity to work with scientifically conducted trials.

Mrs. Garrett had developed, to a high degree, a sort of duality of consciousness. Oliver Fox, writing under the pseudonym of Hugh G. Callaway, used to experience the same phenomenon:

> "I could feel myself standing in the dream and see the scenery (of the astral plane); but at the same time, I could feel myself lying in bed and see my bedroom."

This dual consciousness is characteristic of what the English Master Robert Browning once described to me as *esolepsy*, the ability to turn the mind inwards and to be conscious in two worlds. This forms the basis of the new Yoga which the West is to develop in the Age of Aquarius. It requires the yogin to channel

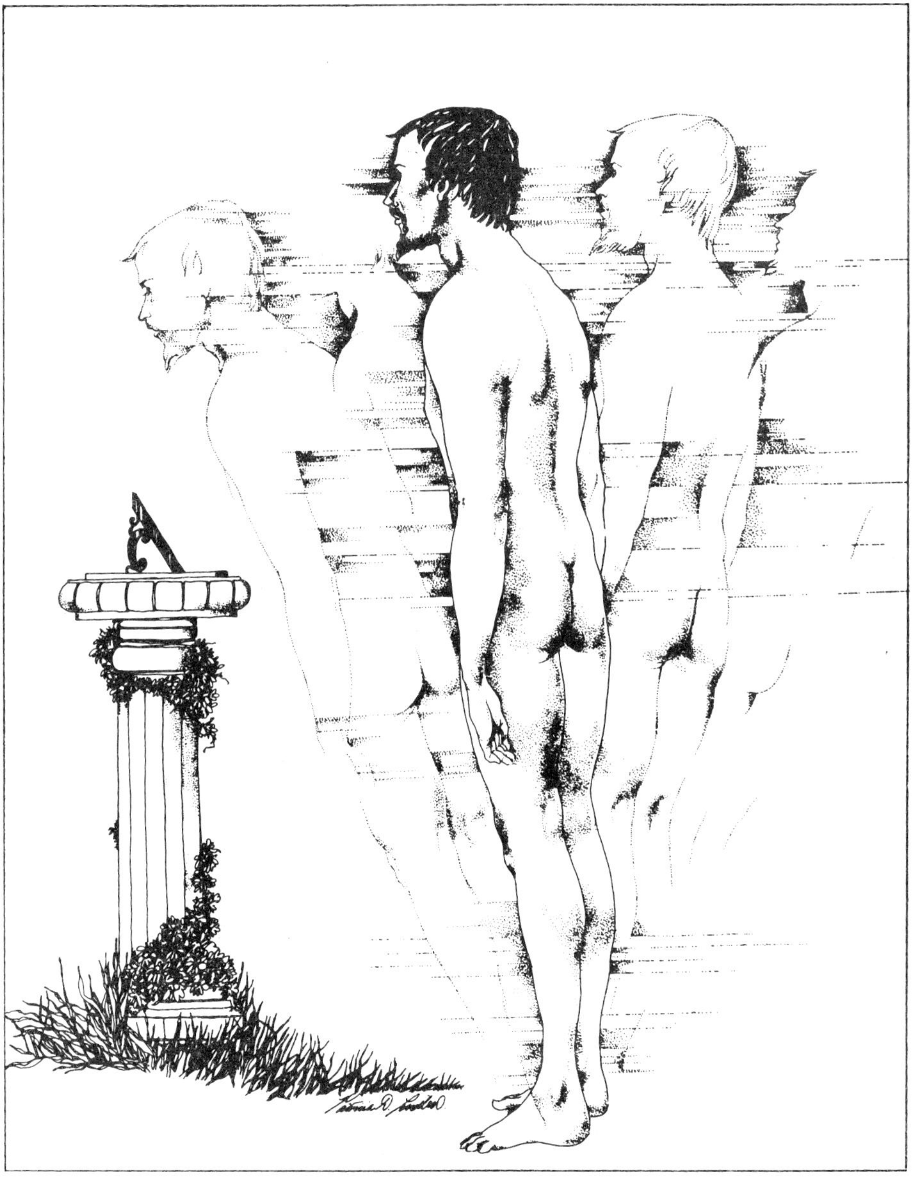

forces from the inner world in which he is also conscious. For those of us who are frontiersmen of the new age, who are pioneering the new Yoga, the observation of common factors of experience in this field is vital. Oliver Fox, Mrs. Garrett and I myself describing physical, mental and emotional symptoms which show that we are on the right track, though our paths are slightly different. There is cataleptic trance whilst esolepsy exists. Those who follow us will have to learn to move their limbs in this state whilst I for my part, can after twenty years endeavour, move only my eyelids and perhaps a finger or two.

In 1932 Mrs. Garrett worked with several well-known psychiatrists and scientists who were then interested in the problem of telepathy and a test was arranged for her in New York:

"I knew for myself," she said, "that in order to accomplish the experiment successfully, I would have to use conscious projection in order to arrive at the destination in Newfoundland which I expected to reach."

Giving an account of her experience, she continues:

"In my projected state in that place in Newfoundland where the experiment was set up, I found myself not only at the place of the experiment, but before I entered the house, I was able to see the garden and the sea, as well as the house I was supposed to enter; I actually sensed the damp of the atmosphere and saw the flowers growing by the pathway. Then I passed through the walls and I was inside the room in which the experiment was to take place. There was no one there and I looked up the staircase, searching for the experimenter I had been told would be there. If I had to move upstairs to find him that would mean additional effort on my part, but fortunately he walked down the stairs

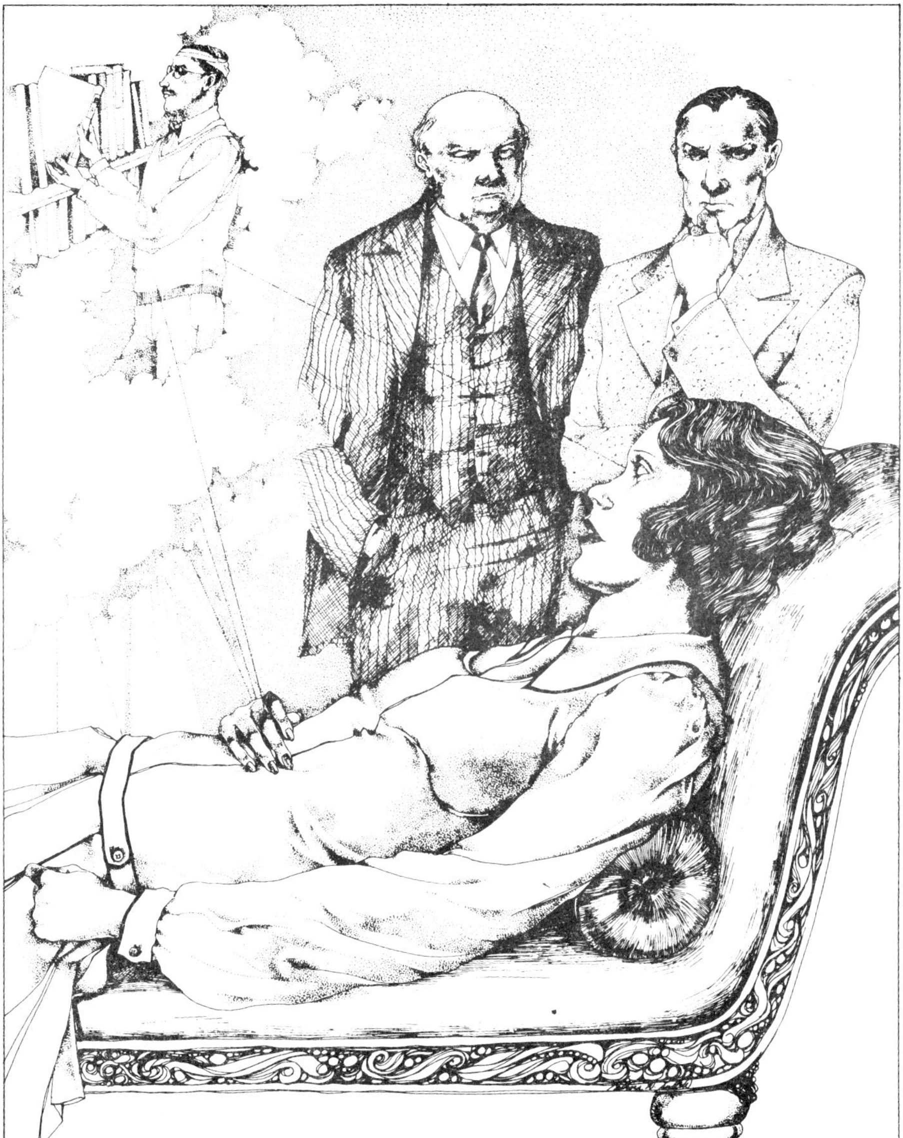

at that moment and entered the room which I knew has been selected for the experiment. What took place then included not only telepathy but the entire range of supernormal sensing, including clairvoyance, clairaudience and precognition. The Doctor, in this experiment, himself had powers of supernormal sensing, and was obviously aware of my presence and that the experiment had begun. In what I am about to relate, the proof of our mutual awareness will soon become evident.

Speaking aloud and addressing me he said: 'This will be a successful experiment,' and I, sitting in a New York room, was able to receive this speech, seemingly through my physical hearing. The investigator in Newfoundland addressed my DOUBLE which I had projected into his study, and said, 'Now look at the objects on the table.' I followed his direction from that moment on, in much the same way as a hypnotised person responds to suggestion.

I could see the objects on the table, not by means of ordinary sight but through clairvoyant vision; I then gave a description of what I saw, to the notetaker with me in New York. I heard the Doctor say, 'Make my apologies to the experimenters at your end. I have had an accident and cannot work as well as I had hoped.' I transmitted what I was hearing in Newfoundland to the notetaker in New York in exact words, which has been spoken to me and I also described the bandage on the Doctor's head.

This had scarcely been done when I heard the experimenter in New York comment, in an aside: 'This can't possibly be true, because I had a letter a few days ago and the Doctor was quite well then.'

The experiment continued and I remained in my projected state: I followed the activity of the investigator in Newfoundland. The next thing he did was to walk slowly to his bookcase in this room; before he reached it I knew that he was thinking of a certain book, and I new its position on the shelf: this was telepathy. He took it down and held it up in his hands with definitely the idea that I, being present could read its title, and he then opened it and, without speaking, read to himself a paragraph out of this volume. The book was about Einstein and his theories of relativity. The paragraph he had selected he read though silently, and as he did so I was able to receive from this mind the telepathic impressions of what he read. The sense of his reading I reported to the stenographer, in my own words, while she sat in the room in New York.

In the meantime, the experimenter, speaking aloud, told me in my projected state, that during this experiment he too had projected himself into the bedroom in New York of the psychiatrist who was his co-experimenter. He proceeded to describe the two photographs that he had actually seen there on this previous visit (physical) to New York but he now explained in Newfoundland that these photographs has been put away, and the bedroom of this friend had been redecorated since his actual physical visit.

This was the end of the experiment and the recorder commented when it was over that the entire proceedings had taken fifteen minutes. Had this experiment rested on telepathy alone I could never have reached nor seen the experimenter, the locality of the room and set-up for the experiment. All that pure telepathy could have produced would have been *the thoughts in the experimenter's mind and the impression of the words he had spoken aloud to me.*

The record of the experiment in New York was posted that night to the doctor in Newfoundland. Next morning a telegram was received from him; in it he described an accident which had occurred just before we had commenced our experiment and a day later a letter was received from him, listing the steps of the experiment as he had planned it. The telegram proved that I had not only heard his message correctly when he spoke to my *double* there, but I had actually perceived his bandaged head . . . From his letter, we had learned he had used a table and placed upon it a series of objects which I had seen correctly by means of *clairvoyance*; every step of my description of his behaviour turned out also to be correct. The book he removed from the shelf, the title and the subject matter he read to himself, were as I described them when received through my own conscious projection and my application of clairvoyance and telepathy."*

The Fifth Stage of Astral Projection

In this stage, the projection is not entirely under the control of the person projecting. He is actively supported by another being who would have to be a Master or an initiate of high order. It is as if a silent watcher intervenes in a subjective experience and takes the situation over, leading it towards a conclusion which is instructive or helpful to the one who projects. It implies that he must be working in an ashram and that he must be a probationary or accepted disciple of a Master. The projection would be part of his training by his elder brothers. The disciple may well be able to manage all the previous stages of projection himself but in this stage, conditions are difficult.

* *Man Outside Himself* by H.F.Prevost Battersby (University Books Inc.)

Here, the target is confused, inaccessible or its locality completely unknown but it is important, for some reason, for him to reach it. Because he requires the help of an adept or an initiate, the moral calibre of the projector must be of a high order, or as a disciple, he must have earned the right to active help through actions in this or a previous life.

One hesitates to give an example from one's own life of such an intimate experience but I have the permission of the silent watcher in this instance to do so. Even still, the astral mission described now will hardly invite credence!

My own early experience of this stage occurred some time about thirty or more years ago. It is recorded in my spiritual diary but I speak from the vivid memory it left with me. I had been pondering over the second to last line of the Great Invocation, "And may it seal the door where evil dwells". The English Master had given me light on other lines and their esoteric implications. I had taken the line as a theme for meditation in the early hours of one morning. Suddenly, having reached an advanced stage of detachment from the physical vehicle, I was aware of a great radiance just behind me and felt a presence. I knew it was the Master, who rarely showed His face in full view. I was gently lifted and suddenly entered full projection. On this occasion, there was no effort on my part. I was able to relax and 'enjoy the view'; I was, in fact, being projected within His aura and with Him. We passed over many lands, not with the abrupt and harsh speed that I normally achieve in long distance travel but with a steady and gentle movement. We passed over valleys and deserts and finally reached a mountainous region. Here, the peaks were bare and dark; there was an atmosphere of gloom which increased as we passed down a gorge and then entered a grotto. The atmosphere became stygian. Evil seemed to fill the air and I was aware that we were in a vast underground hall that grew in size. I could see that a whole civilisation, unlike anything I had ever witnessed, was down there. The people were fair skinned but their hair was dark. Their habitations, clustered in villages on the bare rocks, . . . etc., etc.

To sum up, I had visited 'the place where evil dwells' symbolised by a race of Atlantean degenerates whose practice of evil arts, or what we now call black magic, had helped bring about the destruction of Atlantis. This race still exists, sealed in the bowels of the earth. They are but a remnant now long forgotten but who still live by their occult arts, leaving their underground retreat only in their astral form to prey upon humanity through astral vampirism and possession. We had visited one amongst them, a lone person of spiritual integrity working to bring about some sort of redemption for his fellow beings.

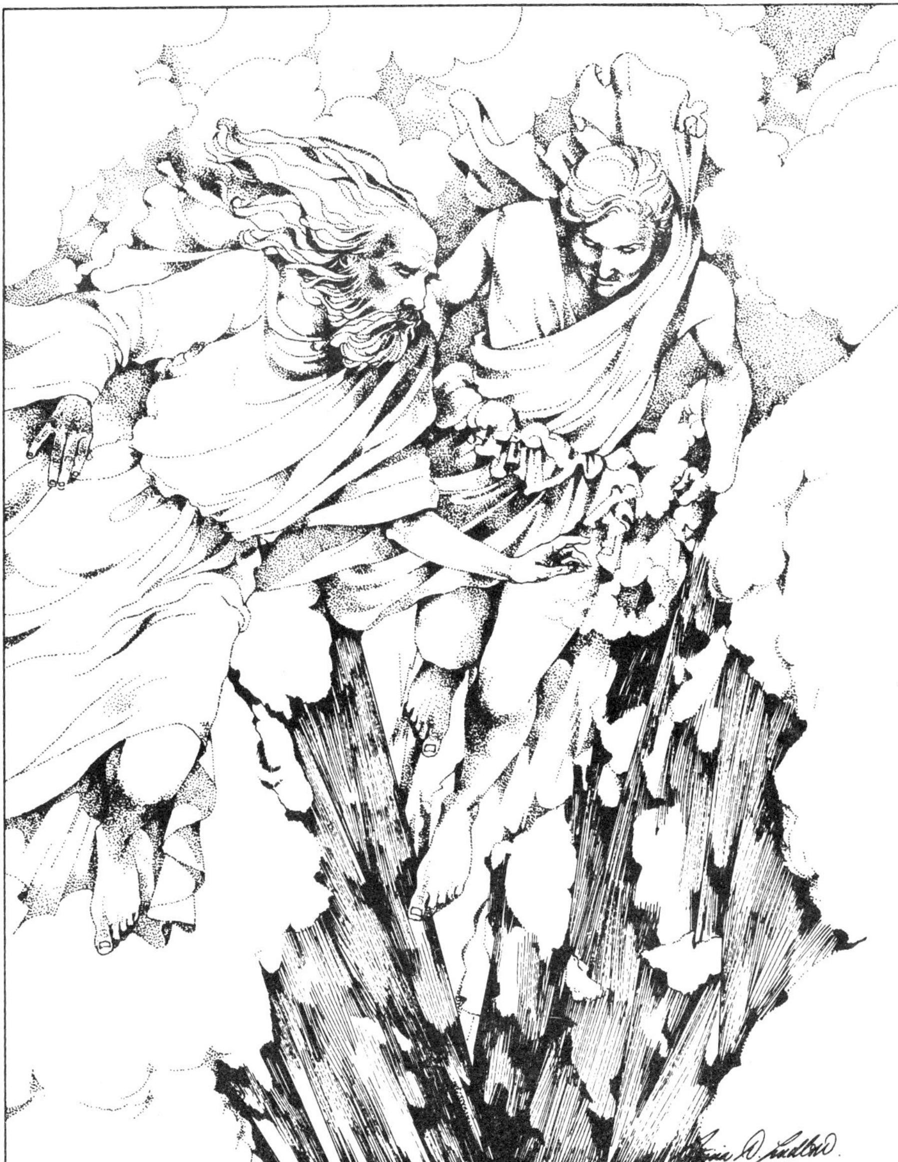

3

THE TECHNIQUES

Technique For Projecting to Stage One

Firstly, read over the description of this stage from the last section so that you know exactly what has to be done. The astral body is to be moved just out of alignment with the physical body. Why should anyone want to do this at all?

The clue lies with sleep. In pure and natural sleep, the astral body is out of alignment with the physical; there is a magnificent rejuvenation and regeneration going on in the inner vehicles whilst the physical body recovers metabolically. We awake completely refreshed and set about our daily tasks once more. But what if we could copy the process at will and in miniature so that at any time, when we needed more energy, we could refresh ourselves in nature's own way?

Many famous people have learnt, in the past, to do just this.

Sir Winston Churchill had just this capacity, to withdraw suddenly from the fatigue of whatever he was doing and in a brief period he could resume once more his arduous tasks at the helm of the British war machine. Emanuel Swedenborg was another. For many years, the author has had the same capacity. It developed slowly, without effort, but he soon discovered the mechanism involved and it forms the basis of the technique used here. The method also is used in some schools of Yoga in Central Europe and, irrespective of results, the process develops spiritual capacities and is, therefore, all the more worthwhile.

The key to the technique is to be found in the effects which resulted from the long automobile drive and the day sailing. In both instances, there were two common factors:

(a) A fatigued body that relaxed rapidly and

(b) A mind that was still alert.

Choose a place on which to lie flat. If you are in an office at your place of work, then lie flat on the carpet. Close your eyes and then do two things. Firstly, *relax yourself rapidly*. This must be done rapidly; as rapidly as you might have done at the end of that long drive in your automobile! It is just as if your body is a sack of corn that is suddenly thrown on to the floor.

The next thing to do is to hold an attitude of rejection in your mind. You must reject, for the time being, the whole world and all its claptrap. Perhaps the telephone has been ringing incessantly, or the paperwork on your desk has been endless.

Say to yourself, "I've just had enough of all this. I'm going to turn inwards for twenty minutes and forget it all!" There is nothing out there that you want and therefore you will not think about anything out there. Your mind will be turned inwards instead. Soon, you will find that your body goes to sleep but your mind should remain alert. The body may even snore! This is self-hypnosis in its truest sense. You have put your body to sleep. After a short period, perhaps as little as five or ten minutes, it will be possible to arouse yourself gently, for your fatigue will have evaporated!

During that time, your consciousness will be outside your body.

It will be in the astral body some few inches above its physical sheath. You may still hear voices in the neighbouring room or noises in the street but it will be with your astral senses! You will now be in a state of astral projection, in full consciousness, a few inches from your usual bodily residence.

Sometimes you may even see the ceiling through your closed eyelids because you are using astral eyes and astral senses and your viewpoint of the ceiling gives you a slightly different impression because you are viewing it from two inches above your head.

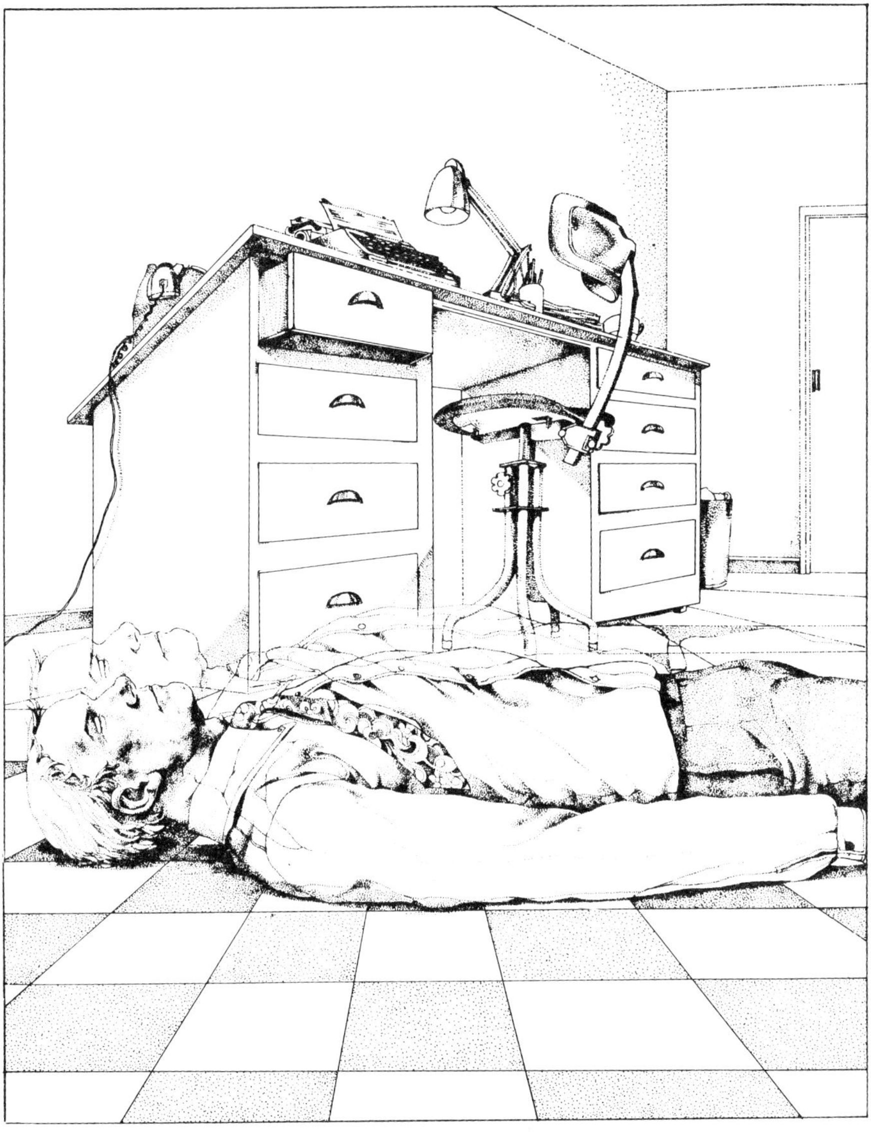

An indication that you are succeeding will be a sudden release of disconnected visual images which Yogis call vrittis. These are the excreta of the relaxed brain and herald the onset of projection. The vrittis are not the first breaths of clairvoyance and when you meet them, you should know them for what they are. Vrittis are thought-forms which constitute part of the brain's excretory mechanism. They are of no esoteric significance except that they are sometimes mistaken for visualisation.

Summary:
Self-hypnosis allows the physical body to slip out of alignment with the etheric. The inner vehicles are then able to charge the etheric. The outcome is energisation of the physical body. Because no sleep has occurred and therefore no break in consciousness, the mind is alert and ready for activity, unlike the usual after effects of say, an afternoon's 'nap'. The inner vehicles have not been projected more than a few inches.

Technique for Projecting to Stage Two

You will remember that, in this stage, the subject finds himself poised above his physical body. This is frequently experienced by a vast section of the population. It is commonly a result of some physical trauma like a motor car accident in which unconsciousness has been enforced when the physical brain is still very much alert. It is characteristic of anaesthesia and may also occur as a prelude to death.

The projection has little occult value except as a proof to some that projection exists. If the subject really wants to project in this way, he could undertake the procedure described under Stage 1 but with a strong thought held in the mind, to the exclusion of all else. The subject might make believe that he is at the bottom of the sea and must force himself to the surface. Strong inclina-

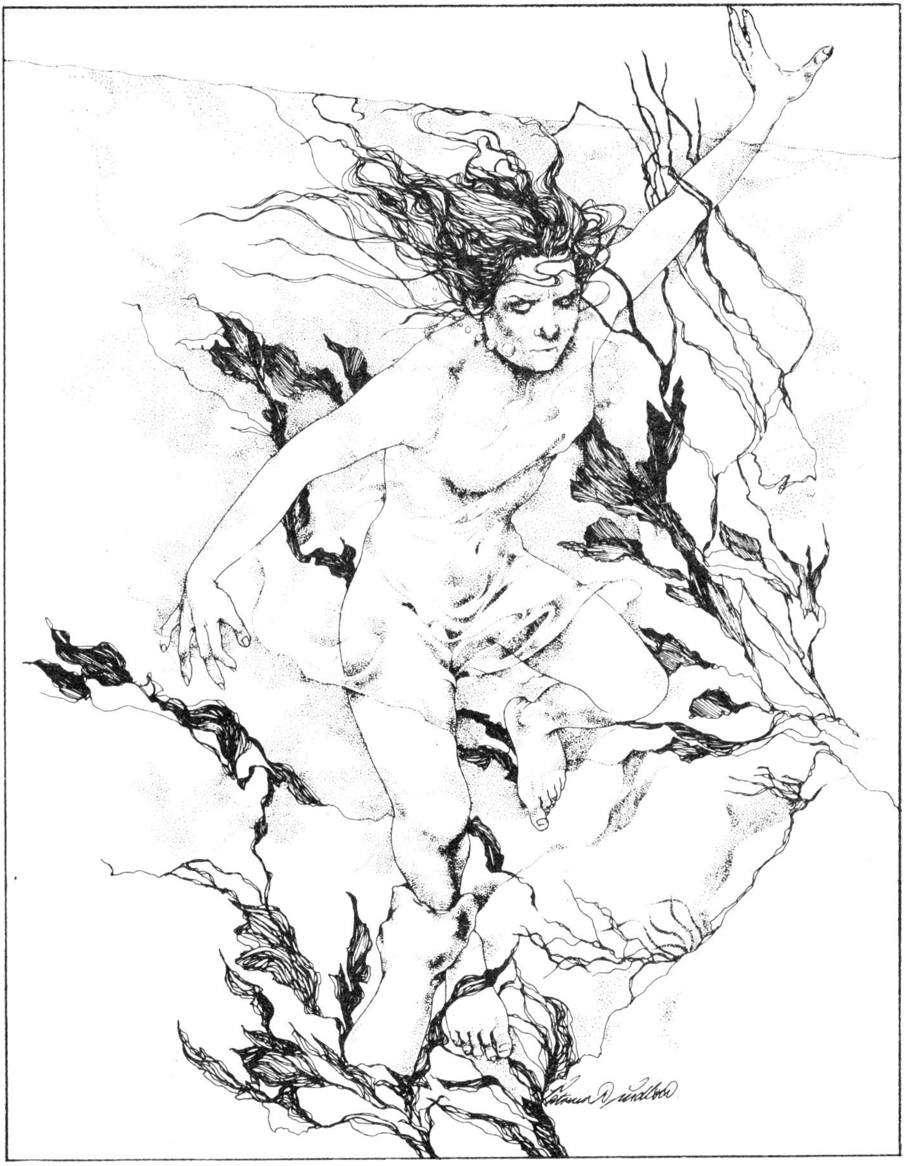

tion to move upwards frequently takes the stage of self-hypnosis one step further and the astral body with a fair proportion of adherent matter hovers above the physical until the propulsive intent is removed, or exhaustion of the physical body draws it back into apposition or coincidence. This stage is never a springboard for more ambitious projection (see picture on previous page).

The determination to move upwards from the Stage 1 projection into the Stage 2 should be as powerful as that which you might summon up if you were at the bottom of a pool and someone was holding you by the ankle under water!

Technique for Projecting to Stage Three

Refer once more to the description of this stage in Section 2. The projection is to a chosen target, a loved one or a loved object. There must be strong desire to be with the target. This impelling desire will ensure success but the nature of the target must be known; it must be visualised and seen clearly at any time in the mind's eye before any sort of projection is attempted. The paramount factors are:

- **Visualisation of the Target** *and*
- **Desire to be with the Target.**

The capacity to achieve adequate visualisation and right desire are elements which, in any case, stimulate force centres in the subtle vehicles which lead to the opening of the Third Eye. Persistence is imperative and rewarding. Visualisation is quite different from imagination though both have the power to manipulate thought substance and thought elementals. Imagination is largely uncontrolled and a negative process stimulated by some sort of sensory input, the sight of something or smell or touch.

On the other hand, visualisation is a controlled, positive process best manifest when the senses are stilled. The words of the poet William Wordsworth are relevant here, when he refers to the Daffodils:

> *For oft whilst on my couch I lie*
> *In vacant or in pensive mood*
> *They flash upon that inward eye*
> *Which is the bliss of solitude.*

It is important that the target be in familiar surroundings, nearby. This is to ensure that when the projection is obtained, it will be in familiar and friendly surroundings. This will obviate fear and distortion. What is seen in the projection can immediately be compared with 'reality' after the projection.

The subject now desires to move his inner vehicles some distance from the physical anchorage. Desire is a paramount factor and Visualisation assumes more importance. It will now be obvious that all physical objects, including the human body, have 'inner' sheaths of mental and emotional substance and that these sheaths attract each other. When we think or Visualise something, we create a likeness of that object in mental and emotional substance which immediately attempts to unite itself with its physical counterpart. If we think powerfully enough and, at the same time, free the inner vehicles from their physical anchorage, then the created thought-form will be drawn to its physical double taking with it our own inner sheaths.

The method is now outlined very carefully . . .

The subject should select some physical object in his home and start to brood over it. An object of art is suitable but it should be one that is attractive to the subject. A marble statuette, a vase, a prism, etc. would fill the role. The object should be studied intensely until you are able to visualise it with your eyes closed at any time. You should also practise 'being with it' in your quiet moments. You should desire to be with it.

The object of attention or target should never be a child in the initial stages of your preparations. Brooding over a child can be injurious to it through the power of your auric emanations.

There are other more suitable inanimate objects. I used a miniature model of the famous statue of David by Michelangelo. I bought one in the city of Florence with which I have karmic links and introduced it into as many aspects of my daily life as possible. Later, projection to the statuette became easy and on several occasions to the real statue as well. Later still, my work with a famous psychologist, Robert Assagioli, in Florence bore fruits. He was centred in Florence.

♦

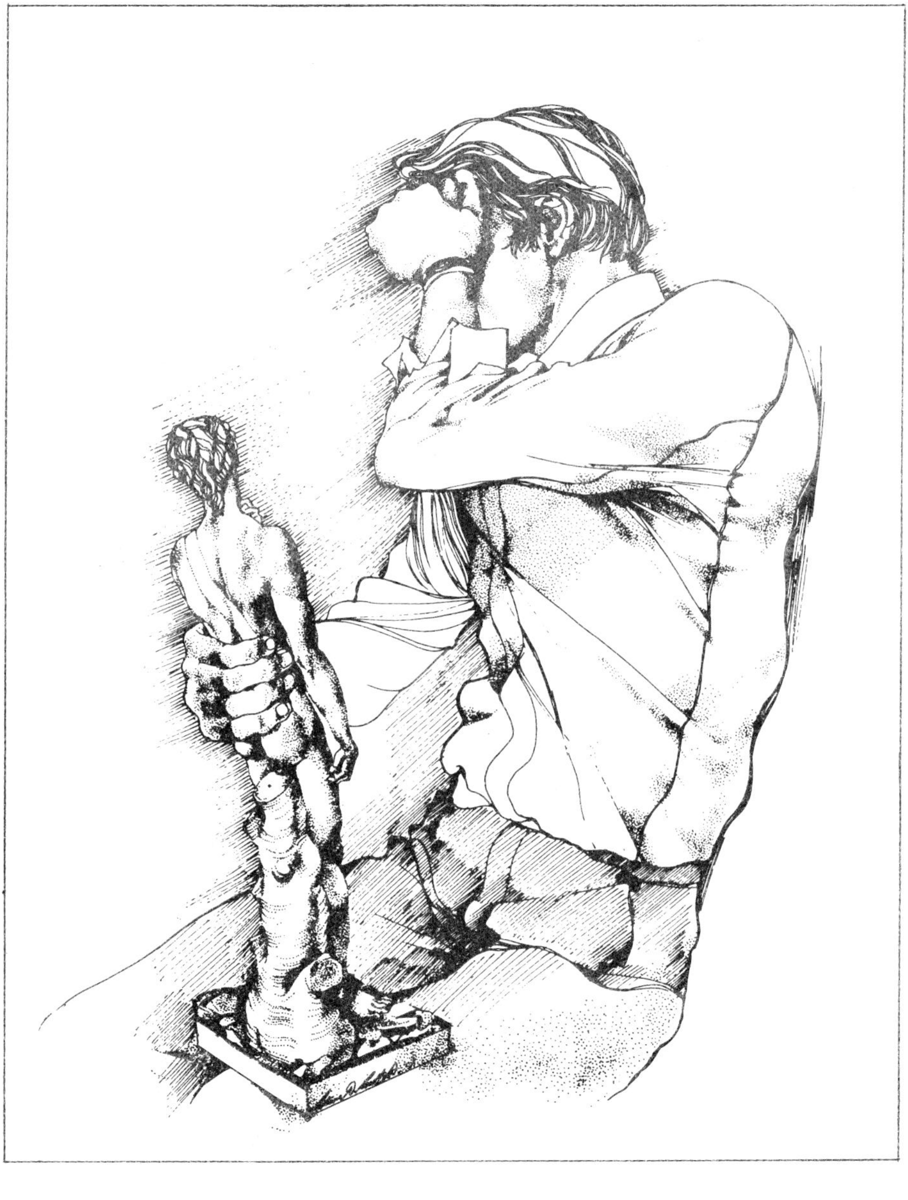

How do we free the astral body from its physical anchorage in this stage of projection? We have learnt a little about this in the first technique but there is a safe and infallible way of obtaining this detachment. Allow the body to go to sleep. But before doing so, *hold the image of the target in your mind.* It must be the very last thought or concern before you sleep. There must also be the accompanying desire to be with the target before you lose consciousness.

If the method is faithfully adhered to, you will, one night confront your target in all vividness of waking reality. When this happens, you should then select another target a little further off. You could either then, project directly to it or project once more to the first target and then, just as if you were moving about in ordinary waking consciousness, you could find your way to the second target.

Thus, for instance, you could start off with a vase in the bedroom, and then move on to the grandfather clock on the landing and then out into the garden to a statuette etc., etc., all the time moving further and further away from the starting point.

◆

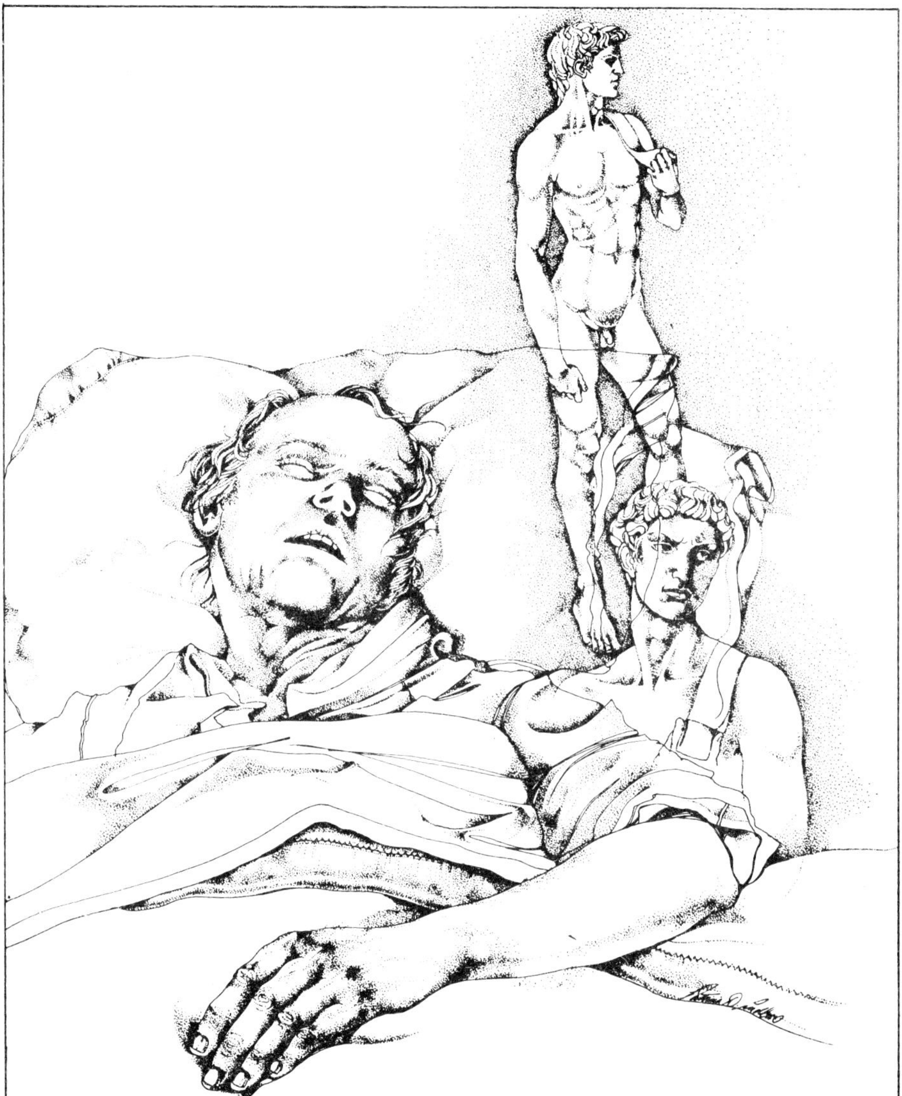

Some Examples

Unconsciously, many objects have formed attachments for me. In my early days of occultism, I once left my watch in a room downstairs when I retired to my bedroom upstairs. Several times in the night, I wanted to know the time but could not be bothered to arouse myself to find out. I built up a desire to be with it and slipping out of my body in an early dream-state, my desire to be with my watch brought about a projection to it. On another occasion, the feint odour of something burning caused me, in a sleep state to visualise my kitchen stove and I projected to it and saw it aglow with fire. I awoke and found that I had left the oven full on.

This last example is interesting. In my projected state, the stove appeared to flow all over. I was seeing it with astral eyes. Later when awake, only the actual hotplate was aglow. Astral vision was different, but not distorted in this instance. On the other hand, the mere presence of a dog in a room, especially if it is enraged can, from an astral viewpoint, distort objects seen about it.

An advantage of this method is that it cultivates many useful and 'healthy' techniques which can be used purposefully in other occult disciplines like meditation. Knowing full well the nature of the object and the setting in which it exists, i.e. your own home helps you to iron out distortions of visual perception in the astral state. Seeing objects in your home from an astral projection is very different from viewing them with normal consciousness. Elimination of undesirable distortions in this early stage helps in more advanced projections later.

Sylvan Muldoon suggests deliberately depriving the body of water to develop a thirst and a *desire* to quench it. This brings about visualisation of a water tap during sleep and projection to it becomes inevitable. I think this is being a bit drastic. The body should not be in any state of imbalance when occult techniques are being practised.

Technique for Projecting to Stage Four

This stage should be the ultimate aim of all; to reach to great distances and, at the target, to carry out activities which constitute a widening of the effective range of one's creativeness. A full description of these creative possibilities is given in Chapter 4.

The technique involved in this stage would be almost a replica of disciplines undertaken towards spiritual evolvement of a high order. No effort is therefore wasted in the practices now outlined. But it must be emphasised that astral projection per se, is not the ultimate for any chela or student of the esoteric. At the worst, it is but a siddhi; at its best, it can give man glimpses of the Fifth kingdom which would spur him on to greater spiritual effort.

There are five prerequisites of success in this stage. Each can be developed or worked on independently. Together, they lead a disciple to the door of initiation and give, incidentally, the full power to project astrally under complete control.

Factor One: The Will

The use of the will becomes increasingly important. Until now, desire has been sufficient to draw the astral body to its target. But, with immense distances involved this process is too slow and cumbersome. It would, for instance, take many hours to reach a target on the other side of the Atlantic if desire only, is the impelling factor. With *will*, it can be done in a matter of seconds. Choose your target and affirm to yourself again and again: "I *will* go there." Concentration and focus are now required far more than mere desire to be with the target.

Factor Two: Reflex Visualisation

In the last technique we saw how important was the factor of being able to visualise the target, to create it, positively, in our minds. This process is taken further here. We must have the concept of the target so well established in our consciousness that we can call it to mind in the flash of a second, anytime and anywhere and by this, I mean even in the inner and subjective world of the dream state!

The power to visualise is pre-eminently the quality of all true poets. It is so tied up with spiritual development that it is no wonder that the ranks of the poets are so often sprinkled with Masters of the Wisdom, adepts and initiates of the highest order.

One has only to read Milton's *Paradise Lost* to see what is meant by 'word imagery' and the power to create in thought substance by visualisation. Milton was a man blinded fairly late in life but it was then that he wrote this, the greatest epic in the English language. The imagery in *Paradise Lost* is unparalleled anywhere except for some lines of a much earlier work, *Lycidas*, in which he describes flowers:

> Throw hither all your quaint enamelled eyes
> That on the green turf suck the honeyed showers
> And purple all the ground with vernal flowers.
> Bring the rathe primrose that forsaken dies,
> The tufted crow-toe, and pale jessamine,
> The white pink, and the pansies freaked with jet,
> The glowing violet,
> The musk rose, and the well-attired woodbine,
> With cowslips wan that hang the pensive head,
> And every flower that sad embroidery wears:
> Bid amaranthus all his beauty shed,
> And daffadillies fill their cups with tears.

Factor Three: Sleeping Lightly

It is quite useless to think of astral projection and activity in the inner worlds if you sleep heavily, without memory being brought through of your dreams and astral life. You may attend church ten times a week but if you are insensitive to what is going on in the inner worlds during the eight hours of your sleep, you are incapable of being instructed or directed by those Great Ones who have your spiritual well-being most at heart. Some of us rush about all day on our various activities until we fling ourselves exhausted on our beds at night. The next thing we know is our alarm clock bringing us back into consciousness. Eight precious hours have been wasted with non-creative and unenlightened inertia. Those hours could have been spent usefully. Everyone is psychic when they are conscious in the astral world. Sleeping lightly brings an awareness of spiritual planes. It is a prerequisite of controlled, efficient astral travel.

It is quite irrelevant to claim that you just cannot remember your dreams or retain any sort of waking consciousness while you are asleep. How many people fall out of bed at night? Very, very few indeed. Why not? They do not fall out of bed because of the consequences! Something within them alerts them to this possibility. That inner consciousness makes them take avoiding action. They are alert to things that concern them!

If the heaviest sleeper was involved in some way in the necessity for sleeping lightly, he would. Many a young man sleeps heavily until he becomes more involved with life. After marriage, with the problems of rearing children, he soon changes. Many such a young husband, thus involved, has learnt to sleep with one ear cocked for the cry of an infant. He knows that if the cry goes unheeded, the other children will be set on aroar and there would be no sleep for anyone!

Oliver Fox's remark, given earlier, is relevant here:

"I could feel myself standing in the dream and see the scenery (of the astral plane); but at the same time I could feel myself lying in bed and see my bedroom."

Factor Four: Development of a Critical Faculty

What is needed here is to develop an awareness that you are dreaming, to become *awake* whilst the body still sleeps.

People say they sleep heavily and yet they *can* be aware of being on the astral plane, or in the dream state if they are sufficiently involved. Who has not had a dream of falling from a step-ladder or a hillside? How many have allowed themselves to hit the bottom? More than sixty per cent of my audiences on lecture tours have had this capacity to awaken themselves from the dream state.

They had an awareness that they were dreaming. Only when a situation threatened them did they act through this awareness and awaken themselves.

Once we are aware that we are dreaming, a whole new world then opens for us, filled with possibilities.

How can we develop this ability to recognise when we are dreaming? We have to train ourselves to develop a critical faculty for recognising that we are dreaming. We must cultivate the ability to appraise a dream, to criticise it, while it is going on. Firstly, we do this after we awaken. We pick the dream to pieces and appraise anything in it which was not true to life, the ridiculous, the traumatic, the impossible. We do this habitually and eventually, when in the dream state, we do it there too, i.e., *keep our minds alert to anything incongruous or absurd in dream content.*

Oliver Fox, writing under the pseudonym of Hugh G. Callaway, makes interesting reading in the light of this technique. He explains how gradually he evolved the conviction that the key to projection was the discovery in a dream that he was dreaming while still holding the waking consciousness at bay, and that this discovery mostly came about by detecting some incongruity in the dream.

Oliver Fox then provides some interesting observations of physical effects noted during the development of this type of technique and ends with a significant observation:

He dreamed that he was standing on the pavement outside his home, viewing the sunlit scene which he knew well, when, as he was about to enter his house, he noticed that the paving stones were not set as he remembered them.

"Then", he writes, "the solution flashed on me: though this glorious summer morning seemed as real as could be, I was DREAMING!

"With the realisation of this fact, the quality of the dream changed in a manner very difficult to convey to one who has not had this experience, instantly the vividness of life increased a hundredfold. Never had sea and sky and trees shone with such glamorous beauty; even the commonplace houses seemed alive and mystically beautiful. Never had I felt so absolutely well, so clear-brained, so divinely powerful, so inexpressibly free! The sensation was exquisite beyond words, but it lasted only a few moments and I awoke."*

---

* from *Astral Projection* by Oliver Fox.

The holding of the waking consciousness and the subconscious at bay, with the freeing of the son of God into bliss and ecstasy of the higher worlds is best symbolised in old alchemical drawings like the one shown opposite.

Summary:
The aim of this development is to become *aware* in your dream state that you are in fact dreaming, i.e. *aware that you are out of your physical body*. All of us have had this experience. Frequently it comes when we experience some violent or repulsive event like falling or coming under attack. Sometimes the dream is so incongruous that the mental faculty, though little present in dream consciousness, revolts. It is this critical faculty that needs cultivation. We do not want to become excessively aroused to awaken fully. But we do want to become aware that such an event is so incongruous or obnoxious that it must be a dream.

Factor Five: Breathing

For reasons explained at the end of this technique, the use of controlled breath can be a powerful adjunct to the success of astral projection to great distances. The student should practise what the Yogis call the *Bellows Breath*. This should be done with utmost regularity for some weeks before the projections are attempted.

The Bellows Breath:
A modification of the breath is used here. The student sits upright but comfortably in a chair out of which he cannot fall (see page 79). He draws air sharply in through his nostrils with such intensity, that they become flared. This is done several times at the rate of about once per second. Do not worry about exhalation. The natural elasticity of the thoracic cage and the lungs will expel the air before the next gasp. Don't do more than *four*

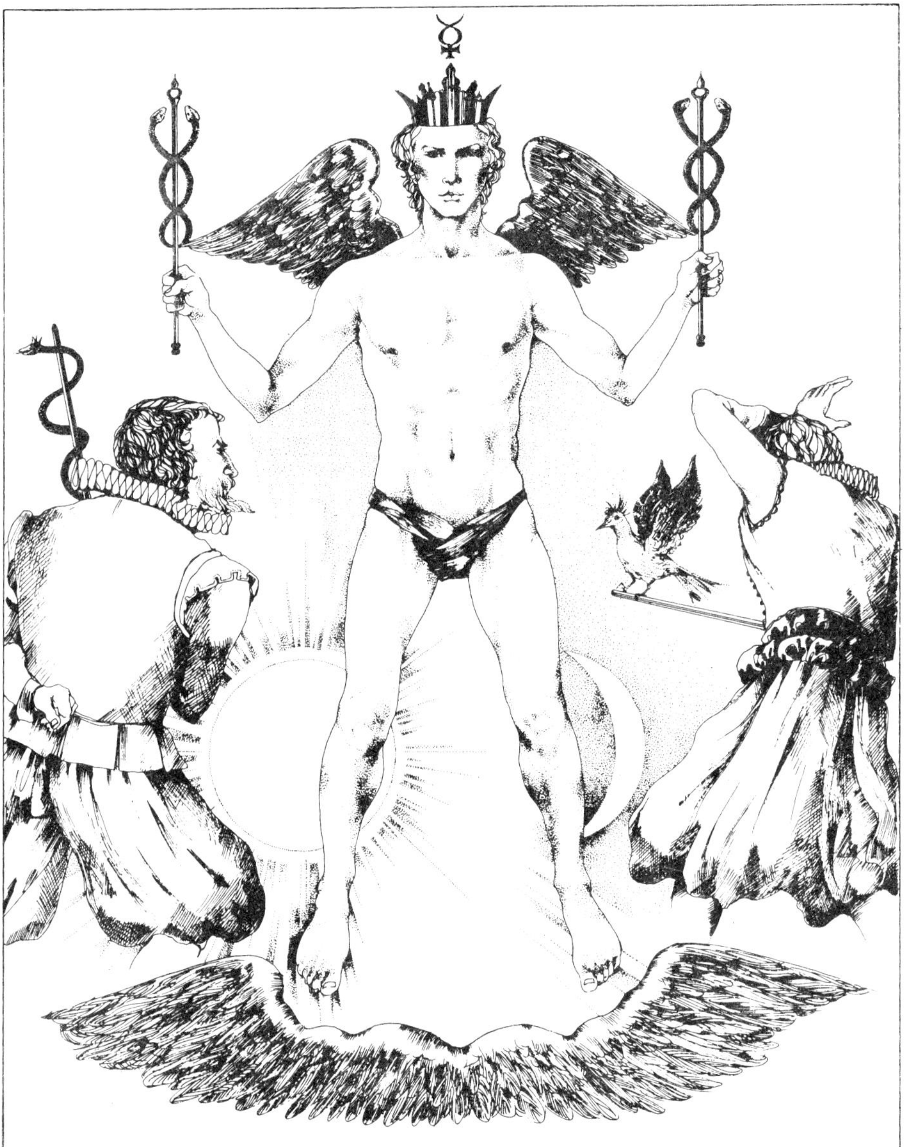

breaths on the first few occasions. Dizziness may ensue. This is the result of minor changes in the blood chemistry and is not dangerous if you are seated. Eventually, you should be able to reach ten or more breaths. This would be sufficient for our purposes but the exercise should be done so regularly that it becomes established as a reflex in your consciousness. There will be no time to sort out breathing exercises in the razor-edged state of consciousness when you are aware that you are dreaming!

The Projection

How are these five factors used? The light sleeper is aware of his dreams. He has developed a critical faculty of perceiving the incongruous in any dream. With this, he soon becomes aware that he is in the dream state, that his physical body is still asleep. He immediately seizes this opportunity to project. He visualises the target and WILLS himself towards it. It is as simple as that. The moment you are aware that you are dreaming, think of your target and will yourself to it. Then, if you wish to have added power to assist you in reaching your target or in maintaining you there, use the bellows breath which you have been practising. This will accelerate your projection and give the whole process increased power. The mechanism of this boost by breathing is dealt with at the end of this section.

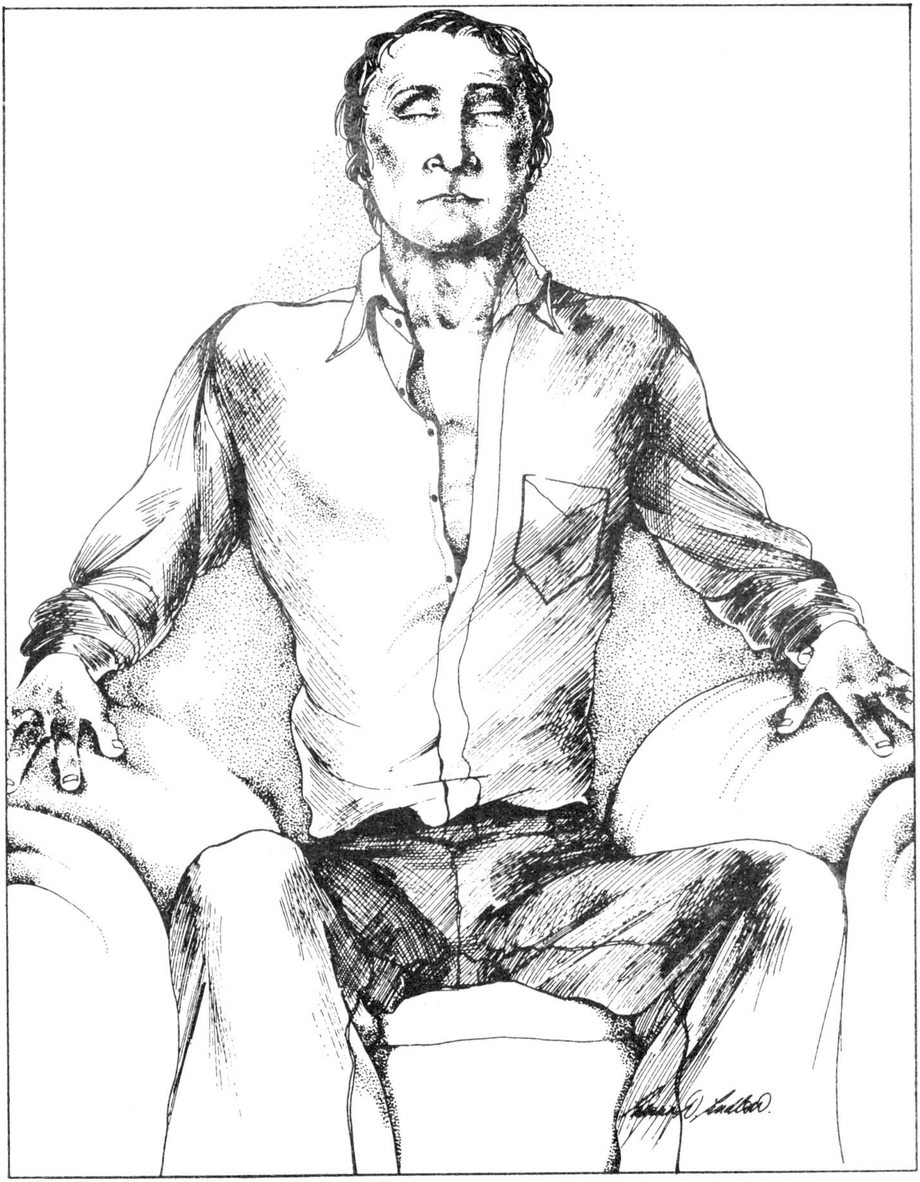

Technique for Projecting to Stage Five

Read carefully the description of this stage in Chapter Two. There is an ancient and true statement about the Path of Initiation:

"The Kingdom of Heaven must be taken by storm!"

Projection is developed as a side-effect of the unfolding of the Third Eye. The neophyte undertakes meditation, study and the service of mankind, persistently and with unswerving courage. He earns the respect of the Silent Watcher, the Master, Who is concerned with his unfoldment. In return for his dedication to The Path he is rewarded with assistance in unfoldment of psychic powers. When he learns that astral projection is but a diversion from his true work and should be employed, in any case, only as part of an act of service to some individual, then he is coached as to special techniques. When he is initiate, he is allowed to project into the Master's presence and to partake of ashramic knowledge and to share in ashramic projects. The basic requirements of this very real technique of astral projection are given in detail in *Superconsciousness Through Meditation*. The catchword here apart from meditation, study and service to mankind is *continuity of consciousness*.

Note on Breathing:

The body left on the bed in repose during astral projection is not just a useless shell. It still breathes and that is a fact of tremendous occult significance. It not only breathes but even though you are in projection you can alter the rate and manner in which it breathes. The body thus becomes a power house of prana and that power can be drawn upon, in ways we cannot yet say. But during projection, if the bellows breath is used vigorously, the astral body becomes more powerful and more easily controlled.

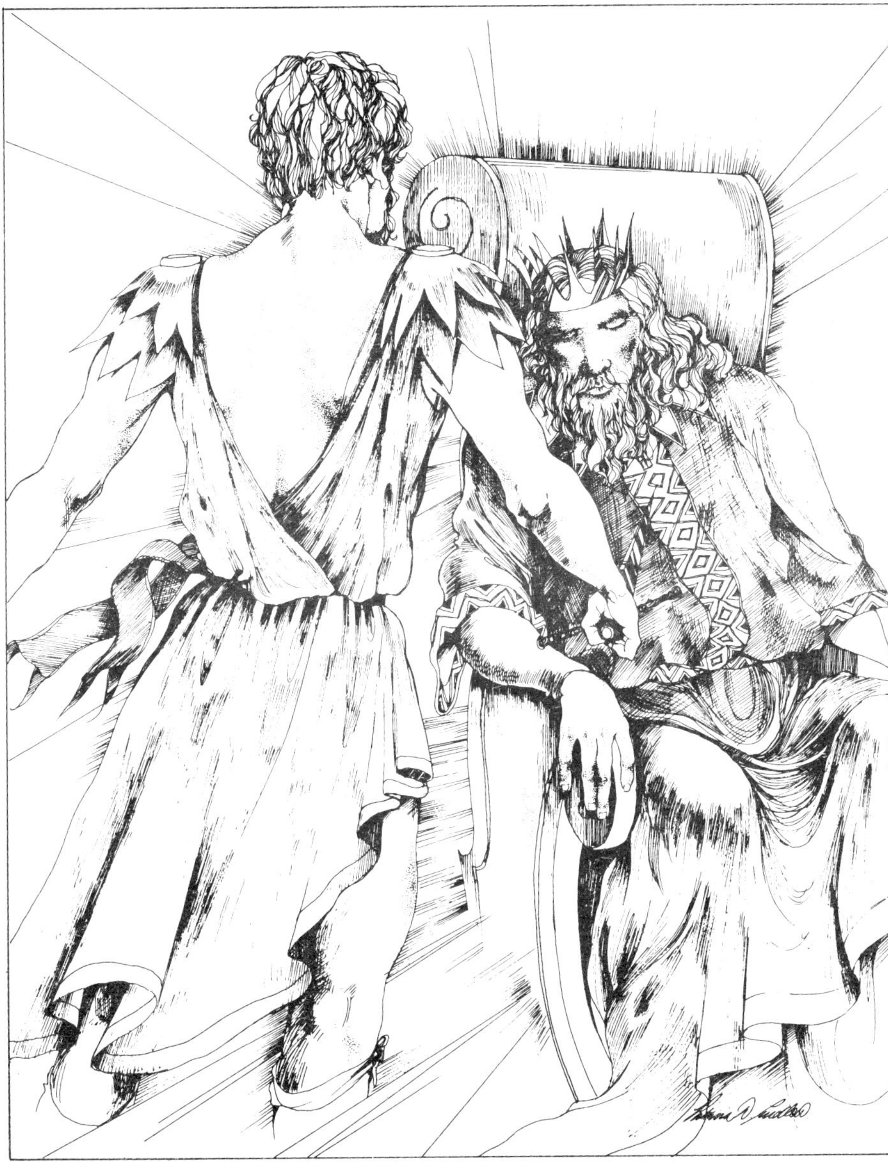

The bellows breath will help you hurtle through the ethers, maintain you in any target area and help you to ward off any astral attack.

The information given here has never previously been made available to the public, but the time is right.

4

THE ASTRAL WORLD

THE ASTRAL WORLD

We are so used to thinking of our own world as tangible and solid that it comes to us as a bit of a shock when we project into a world where gravity is unreliable, where forms change even as you think of them and where the dead and departed are as familiar as if nothing had ever separated them from us.

The astral world is made of emotional substance and when any man or creature feels, he creates substance of an astral denseness in the astral world. This becomes quite a thought when you think of men, perhaps thousands of them at any one moment, dying in pain or horror on some battlefield and all contributing to the sensitive world of astral forms. Thus, the astral world is made up of astral or feeling-matter of various orders or planes. In the lowest of the astral planes, the substance of those planes would correspond to the low and negative vibrations of feelings like horror, fear, hate, anguish, lust, etc.

Correspondingly, in those planes of the astral world live astral, human forms of a similar order. Here would gather the felons of real life, the rapists and all men of vicious character. There is no truer expression than "birds of a feather flock together" than in the astral world. This is why the teachings of the Catholic Church are so accurate in many of their descriptions of places like Purgatory and Limbo, etc. These places exist as certainly as do the equally glorious planes of the highest astral worlds, the planes of Heaven of the Christians, the Paradise of Islam, the Valhalla of the Norsemen, the Summerlands of the Red Indian, etc. They are all there and peopled accordingly to race, to their karma, to their spiritual development and a host of other factors.

In the long struggle of the disciple towards ultimate reality, it is inevitable that every single son of God must experience all these planes. Even the great man, Emanuel Swedenborg, visited Heaven and Hell and left us glorious records of his experiences.

Whatever a man thinks or feels, is recorded in astral form somewhere in the astral world. The characters of Charles Dickens exist in the astral world! Every time a man reads about a character of Dickens, like Mr. Pickwick, he energises under the maxim of 'Energy Follows Thought', the astral body of Mr. Pickwick.

When we laugh with Mr. Pickwick, or cry with Mr. Pickwick, we are sending strong emotional energies into the astral world that will feed the astral form of Mr. Pickwick so that its existence may be prolonged until the very last memories of Charles Dickens' immortal character are lost in history. Then the 'umbilical cord' linking the character to the physical world will be severed and the astral shell of Mr. Pickwick will evaporate.

Perhaps this is well illustrated by an experience I have had many times in the astral world. On one occasion, being a lover of gardens and flowers, I was wandering down a garden path in the astral world. There, I saw the most beautiful flowers of every description. Not the least of these were the roses. I took one and cupped it in my hands, saying to myself, "Oh, what a gorgeous bloom!" Immediately, as I stared lovingly at it, the flower was transformed. It grew and grew until it was a giant in proportion to other blooms. With my sustaining attention or directed love energies, it had waxed and flourished, whilst others which were not similarly blessed, were unaffected.

Thus, from this example, we can see the effect of our loving or our hateful thoughts on those images of things or of *people*, that exist in the astral world but, which, in many instances, have physical counterparts in our own world!

This fact, that Man creates with his thoughts and feelings in the astral world shows the truth in the occult statement that Man is a 'god in the making'. It shows that we can be supremely creative

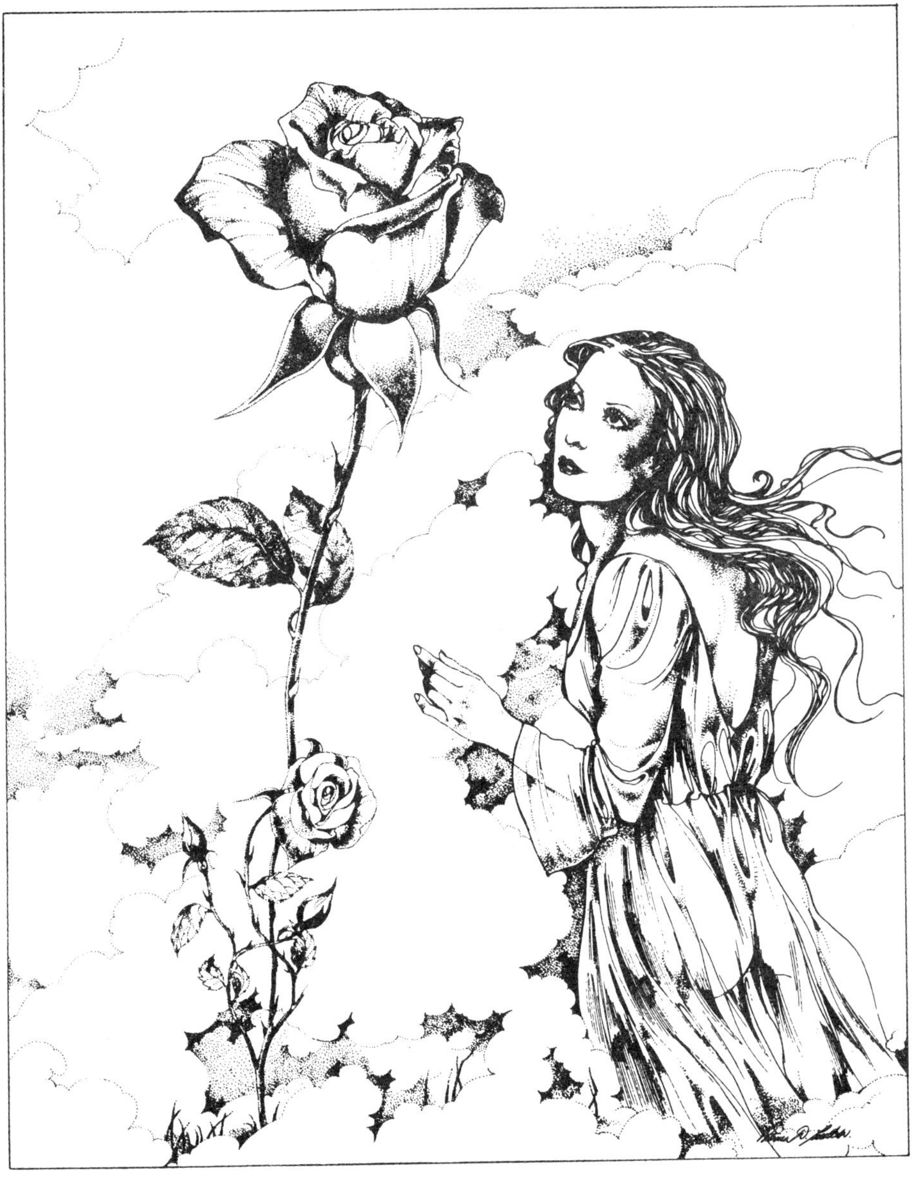

and that in astral projection, we get the opportunity to see and even examine what Man makes in the inner worlds. We will see there country roads, beautiful houses, slums, gallows, prisons and factories. But we will also witness another phenomenon. Man also creates, unwittingly, images in the astral world of all those things which he hates or loves, fears or desires and these creations of his very own remain in contact with him by the same sort of umbilical cord mentioned earlier. Every image that he creates has its counterpart in the astral world. Let him fear spiders, and one kind of spider in particular, then there will appear, in astral matter, the very spiders he abhors and these real beings will always hover in his proximity whether he be awake or asleep. Whenever he fears them powerfully, he will feed them new life. If he, by nature, is a sensitive or clairvoyant, he will be pestered by these images, which together form what is called 'The Dweller on the Threshold'. If, in addition to the above, he produces a small amount of ectoplasm, especially when he is in a state of fear and anguish, and if the room is darkened, he will materialise images. Many children fit into this category. A child, at night, should never be denied a light in his room if he is at all sensitive to 'seeing things in the dark' or to nightmares. A light will prevent such experiences for, as stated earlier, white light dissipates ectoplasm.

The great writer of the occult, Bulwer Lytton, speaks of the Dweller. In his famous occult classic, *Zanoni*, he describes a confrontation of a neophyte with his Dweller. No man may take the third Initiation without confronting his Dweller, facing up to its challenge and destroying it. He destroys it when he knows it for what it is, an illusion constructed out of his own fears.

Oscar Wilde refers to the Dweller in his book, *The Picture of Dorian Gray*. The dweller there, takes the form of a portrait in oils on to which in inflicted all the fears and crimes committed by an ageless youth.

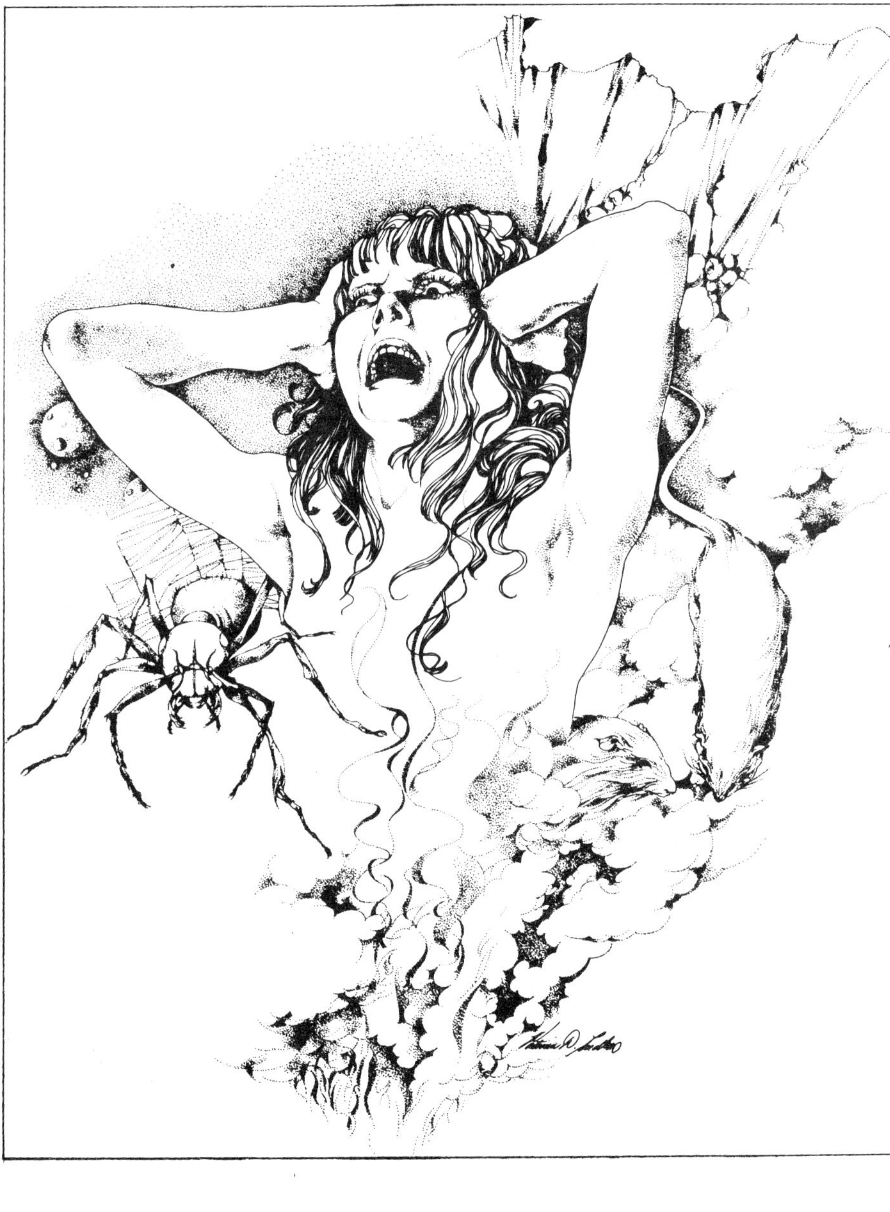

We saw earlier how important was the factor of Breath. Properly regulated and used at the correct moment, it can give astral projection the added impetus it needs when creative acts are demanded of one in the inner worlds.

We sometimes overlook the fact that the sounding of a word also involves the use of breath. The spoken word gives rhythm and control to the exhaled breath. No wonder then that words of famous mantrams, prayers, epic poems and songs of a patriotic nature, when used on the astral plane, produce situations pregnant with power.

The writer has used the Lord's Prayer on many occasions with powerful results. The words, "Thy Will Be Done On Earth As It Is In Heaven', triggered off many an experience which, in some instances, led to bliss, ecstasy and visual experiences, such as that depicted in the illustration.

The sounding of the Aum, whilst in full awareness in the inner planes, brought me mystical experiences of an oriental flavour.

Man can perform many acts of service when in astral projection. On one occasion, I came across a group of bewildered people in the astral world. They were the victims of an air accident. Around them, lay the scattered remnants of their plane still smouldering. The survivors were huddled, frightened and weeping on the side of the mountain that had wrought the havoc. I called to them to have no fear, telling them they were the victims of an accident and that there was nothing to fear for they had, as they could see, survived death. But my words only made them more fearsome and their terror grew. I turned away from them very abashed at my clumsiness.

Then suddenly, I once again felt that radiance behind me and knew the Master Robert Browning was close at hand. A powerful force took hold of me and swung me around once more to face the

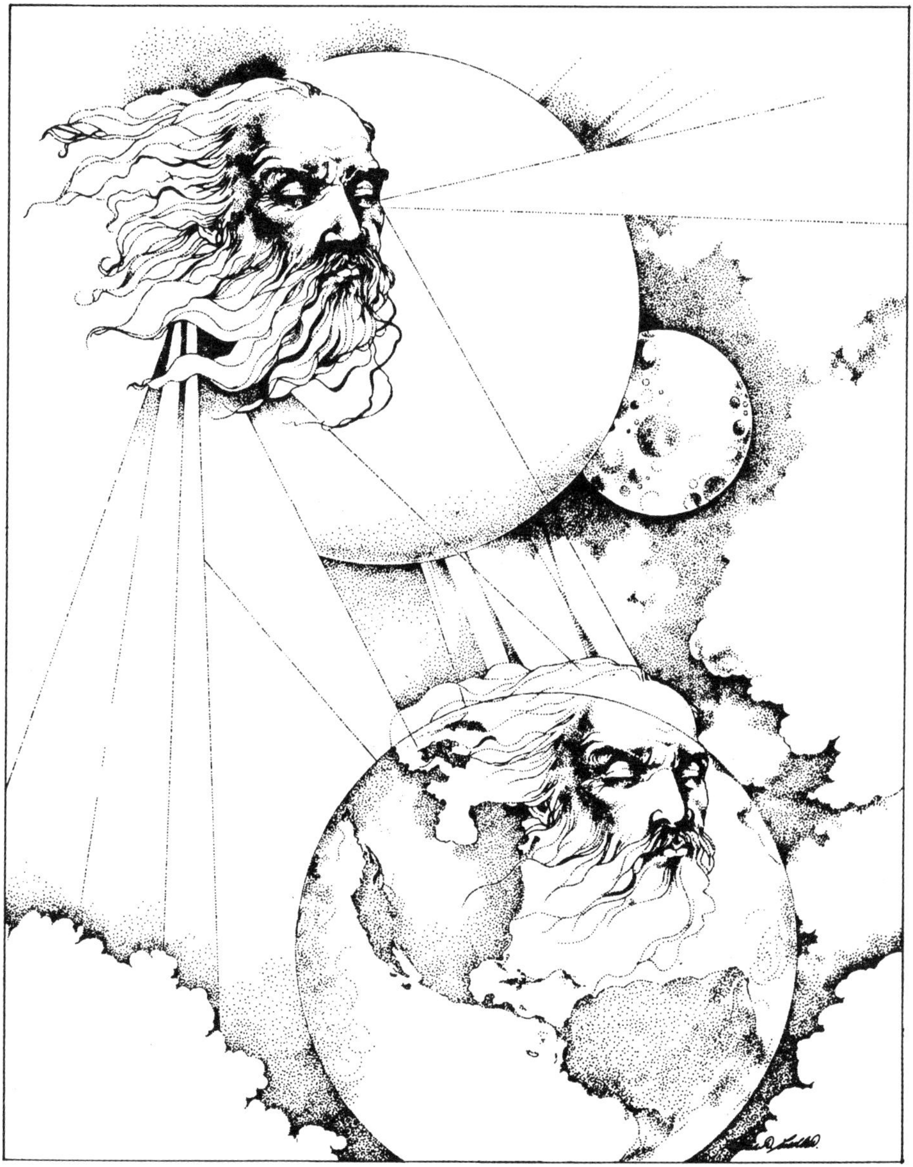

huddled group. I found myself making the sign of the cross to them, something quite alien to my makeup! As I did so, great sheets of white light shot through me towards them. Their faces lit up and I found myself saying the Lord's Prayer. Afterwards, they rose to their feet with happy and loving looks at me, though I had, of my own accord, done nothing, and they went off happily towards the West where there was a lighted area now visible.

Even with the help of a Master, one is not always quite so successful in acts of service in the astral world.

Helping aged people to leave their disease-wracked bodies by coaxing them upwards and out of them during their sleep state, or death coma, is another service that is in constant demand of one roaming the inner worlds in full consciousness.

Without the help or approval of the Master, one's actions can become distinctly hazardous or unpleasant.

Many years ago, in South Africa, I was asked by a friend of mine to go and talk to his brother who was in Pretoria Jail awaiting the death penalty. Marcus Werthen had been sentenced to hanging for the murder of a bus conductor. I saw him only half-an-hour before he was hanged. In that short space of time, I talked to him about life after death and the sort of survival one experiences in the astral world. He had, until then, never heard a word from anyone about these matters and, after his first uneasiness, he became absorbed in what I had to say. I told him he would survive the moments after the noose tightened.

Very foolishly, I suppose, and in my enthusiasm to help, I offered to reach him in the astral world after his death. I told him to try and hold an impression of my face strongly in his mind and I promised I would project to him as soon as possible, allowing a few days for the trauma of the experience to wear off.

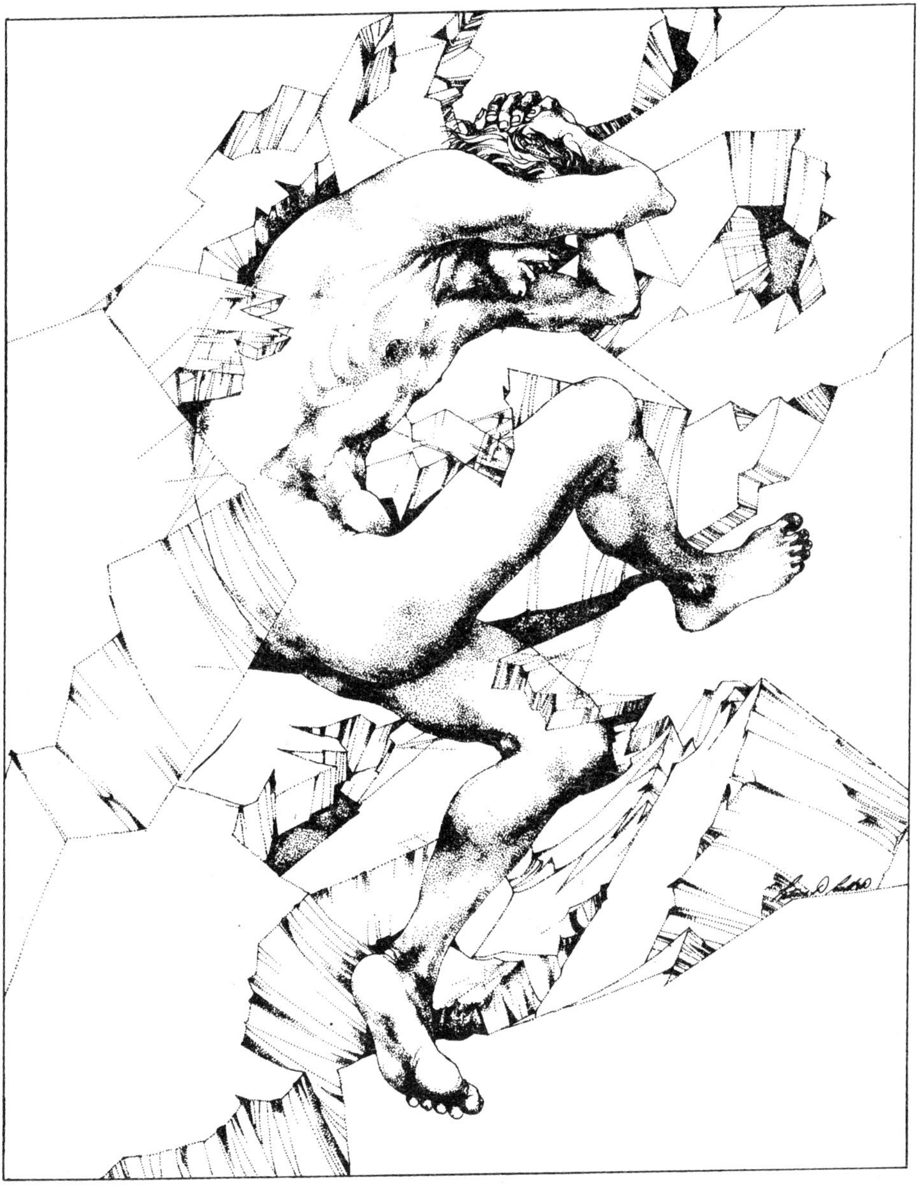

Some nights later, when I was alert in the astral world, I projected towards his image. As I fought my way through the ethers, I encountered such opposition to my movements as I never wish to experience again. The most appalling vibrations threw me about. It was just as if I were fighting my way through a river of iceflows! I was somersaulted and thrown about relentlessly and my determined will and breath could not bring me to my target. Whether I was not meant by my ashram to be involved in such service work or whether the vibrations of the plane now inhabited by Marcus Werthen were too heavy for me, I do not know, but I never reached him then and did not dare try again later.

The ways in which a man might be more creative by having access to the inner worlds in full consciousness are innumerable. It would depend, to a great extent, on the qualities of his Rays, as it did in my own instance I had taken a degree in politics at university: I was most interested in the affairs of nations and in social and economic problems. Very early in the sixties, I became aware that the Master R.B. did not favour England's entry into the Common Market at that time. I meditated on the subject for some time and came to the conclusion that He was right and that England should *not* enter it.

I immediately threw my own mental resources into the fray. A whole group of us, centred about the English Master, directed our thoughts against entry. Whether or not we were responsible, at least in part, for the unaccountable opposition of General de Gaulle to entry, the reader must judge for himself. But on many occasions projection to General de Gaulle and the directing of powerful thought suggestions at him, when in his presence astrally, certainly appeared to me to have effects. How much stronger must not have been the directed will of Robert Browning in this matter, He who was once, as King Henry V, the victor of Agincourt!

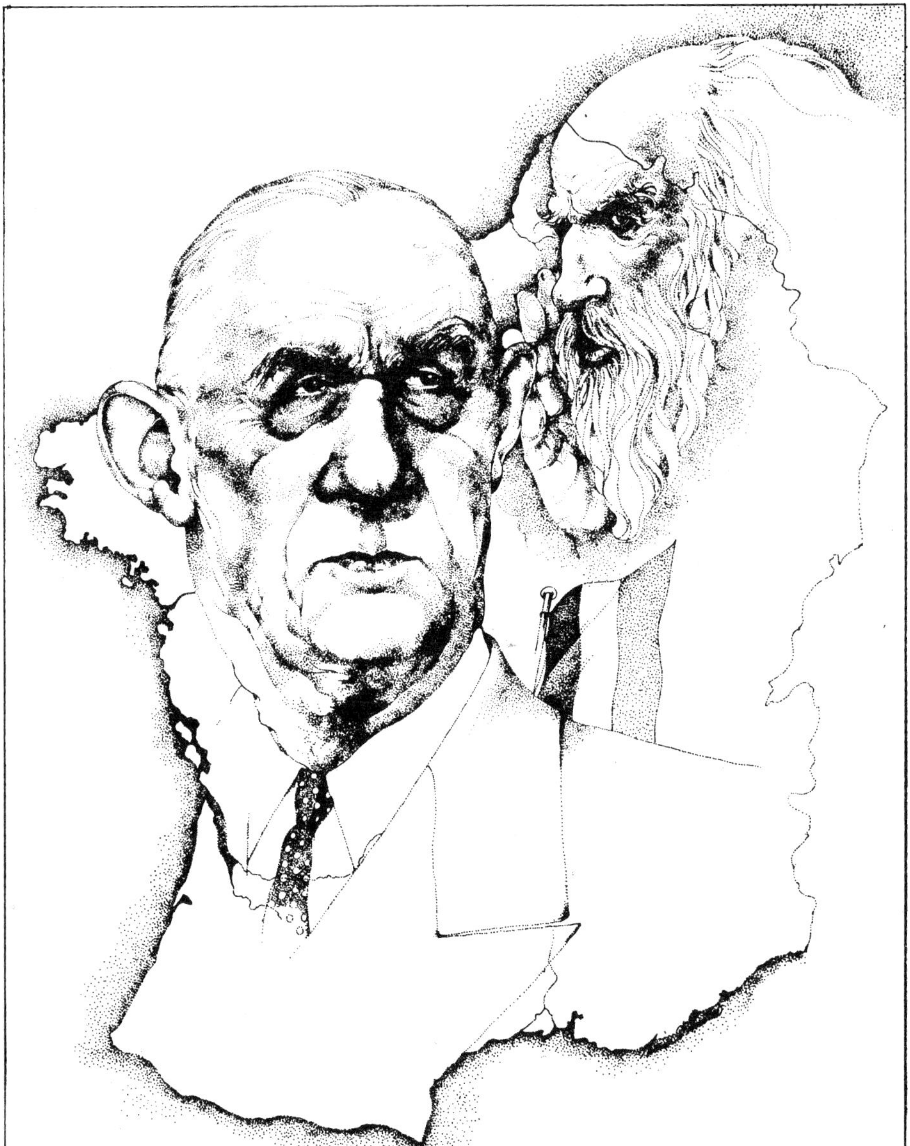

As the world knows, France delayed again and again before giving consent to Britain's entry.

Equally so, might others be able to intervene in World affairs when necessary. The calming of an agitated dictator, like General Amin of Uganda or the stimulation of interest in royalty as to the plight of some others of their subjects; all these have been possible in astral projection.

There is yet another reason for becoming astrally conscious. There is to be an attempt, at the end of this century, beginning, it is said, about the year 1975, to restore the Mysteries and, it is also said that the Masters will "walk amongst us!" In Their coming, they will first be contactable on the astral plane and this offers an opportunity to many a neophyte to become powerfully aware on that plane in order to assist Their work!

The Sexual Factor in Projection

If the desire factor must be strong in astral projection, it is inevitable that some desires will be sexually inspired. There are many examples of this which are implied if not admitted. But there is fortunately, a factor which acts in conjunction with sexual desire that makes astral projection with sexual intent unrewarding.

All men know that the male dream life is often filled with sexual themes. They also discover, very quickly, that the culmination of a sexual theme to its logical conclusion in orgasm and ejaculation cannot be accomplished *without waking*. The sharpness of sensory feeling on the astral plane of the dream world is nowhere near to the refined and exquisite capacity of the physical plane to feel. A man has to come through to physical wakefulness to complete his sexual experience.

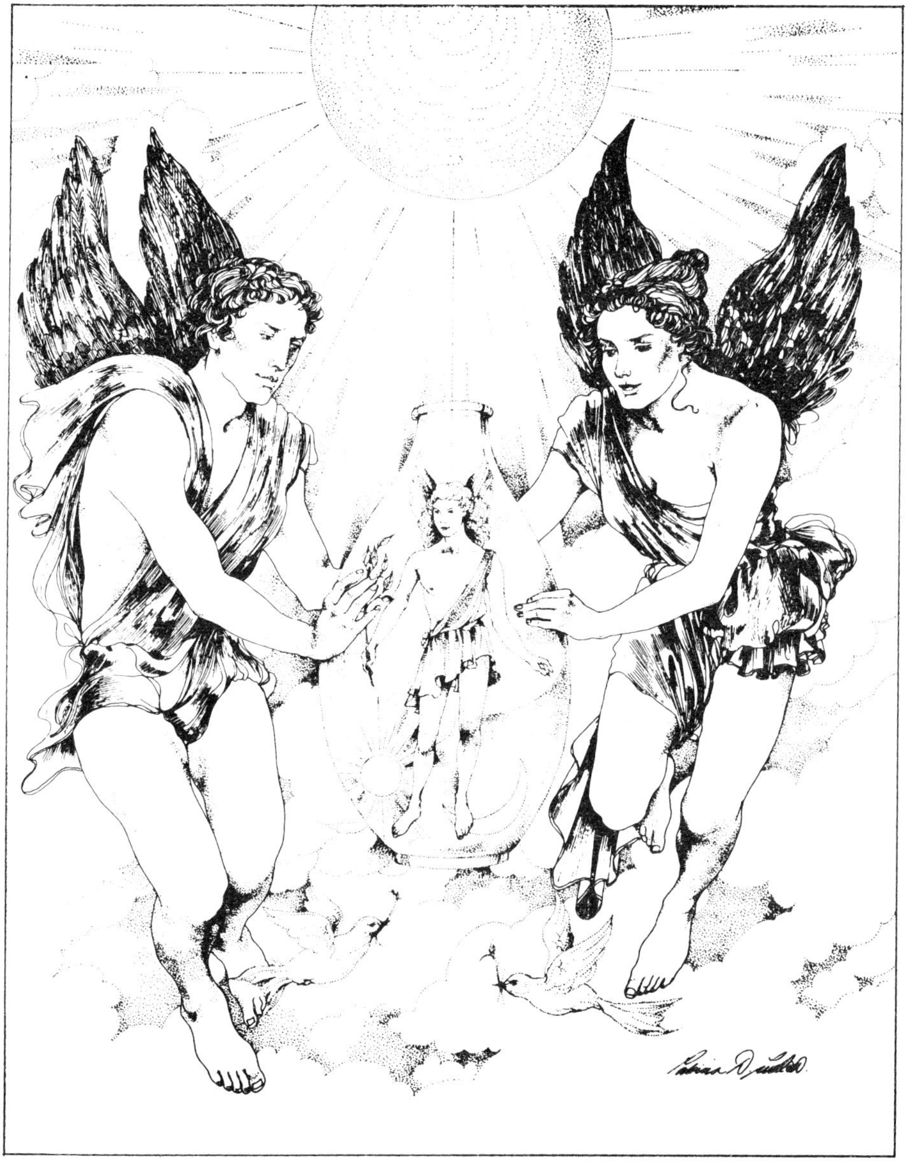

This consideration is important because experimenters in astral projection report that if temptation is not resisted, there is a hasty return to the physical body. An example of this is quoted here from *Life and Action:*

"In April 1913, I was, for about a month, Captain of the gunboat Marietta, and was lying alongside the dock in Brooklyn, N.Y. My wife remained at the house in the Naval Yard at Boston. One night I returned to the ship, from the city, at about 11 o'clock, went to the cabin, and in due time, retired to my stateroom and went to sleep in my bunk.

During sleep I *was conscious that I had left my physical body* and travelled with seeming great speed over, but some distance above the ground to Boston, where I sought my own room and took my accustomed place in bed.

Here after a while, I was conscious that my wife had placed her hand upon my shoulder, and I made a strong effort to turn over and respond to her touch. This effect seemed to cause me to leave the bed and room and return over the same route to New York at the same speed, and thereupon I reoccupied my bunk on board ship and awoke.

At once, it occurred to me that this must be an experience, so I reached out and switched on the electric light and noted the exact time. The next day, I wrote to my wife and, without telling her anything about my experience, I asked her if she had noticed anything during the night in question.

Her reply was that she strongly felt that I was in bed, and had reached out and touched me on the shoulder! So real did it seem to her that she sat up to investigate, and finding nothing, thought nevertheless that she would make a note of the time, which she did, and the two times, hers and mine, were identical."

THE ASTRAL WORLD

Both Sylvan Muldoon and Oliver Fox describe how, yielding to the irresistible temptation (irresistible, at least, to their astral forms) to attract the attention of a charming lady, had sent them hurtling back to their physical moorings. (*Man Outside Himself*, by H.F. Provost Battersby, University Books).

Bibliography

Fox, Oliver: *Astral Projection*. Citadel Press, New York, 1993.

Garrett, Mrs. Eileen: *My Life as a Search for the Meaning of Mediumship*. London and New York, 1939.

Muldoon, Sylvan: *The Projection of the Astral Body*. London, 1929, 1939, 1950, 1961.

Powell, Arthur E.: *The Etheric Double and Allied Phenomena*. London, 1925.

Shirley, The Hon. Ralph: *The Mystery of the Human Double*. (1938). University Books, New York, 1965.